Bob
No Ordinary Cat

About the Author

James Bowen is a street musician in London. He found Bob the cat in 2007 and the pair have been inseparable ever since.

Dedication

In loving memory of Graham Jenkins and Jane Marguerita Howden, and dedicated to everyone else who has given us their absolute continual support. Without all of you we wouldn't be here now.

Bob
No Ordinary Cat
James Bowen

HODDER

First published in Great Britain in 2013 by Hodder & Stoughton
An Hachette UK company

2

Copyright © James Bowen and Garry Jenkins 2013

A CIP catalogue record for this title is available from the British Library

Paperback ISBN 978 1 444 76490 1
Ebook ISBN 978 1 444 76492 5

Typeset by Hewer Text UK Ltd, Edinburgh
Printed and bound by CPI Group (UK) Ltd, Croydon, CR0 4YY

Hodder & Stoughton policy is to use papers that are natural,
renewable and recyclable products and made from wood grown
in sustainable forests. The logging and manufacturing processes
are expected to conform to the environmental regulations
of the country of origin.

Hodder & Stoughton Ltd
338 Euston Road
London NW1 3BH

www.hodder.co.uk

Contents

Chapter 1
Fellow Travellers

There's a famous quotation that says we are all given second chances every day of our lives, but we don't usually take them. I spent a big chunk of my life proving those words. But all that changed in early spring 2007, when I befriended Bob.

I first met Bob on a gloomy Thursday evening in March. There had been a hint of frost in the air that night, which was

1

why I'd arrived back home in north London a little earlier than usual after a day busking around Covent Garden.

The lift to my flat wasn't working, so my friend Belle and I headed towards the stairs. The light was broken and the hall was dark, but I couldn't help noticing a pair of glowing eyes in the gloom. A ginger cat was curled up on a doormat outside one of the ground-floor flats. He was a tom – a male.

He fixed me with an intelligent stare. 'So who are you and what brings you here?' he seemed to say.

I knelt down. 'Hello mate. I haven't seen you before. Do you live here?'

He kept looking at me, weighing me up. I stroked his neck, partly to make friends and partly to see if he was wearing a collar. He wasn't.

He was enjoying the attention. His coat was patchy and bald and he was clearly hungry. From the way he was rubbing against me, I could tell that he needed a friend.

'I think he's a stray,' I told Belle.

Belle knew that I loved cats.

'You can't have him, James,' she warned. She nodded at the doormat he was sitting on. 'He probably belongs to whoever lives here.'

Belle was right. The last thing I needed in my life just then was a cat. It was hard enough taking care of myself.

The next morning the cat was still there. I stroked him again. He purred away, enjoying the attention.

In the daylight I could see that he was a gorgeous creature. He had a really striking face with piercing green eyes. Judging from the scratches on his face and legs, he must have been in a fight or an accident. His coat was thin and wiry and he was covered in bald patches. I was genuinely worried about him.

Stop worrying about the cat and worry about yourself instead, I thought. Reluctantly I headed off to catch the bus to Covent Garden, where I was going to try and earn a few quid busking.

When I got home it was late – almost ten o'clock. I hurried to the corridor where I'd seen the ginger tom. He'd gone. Part of me was disappointed, but mostly I felt relieved.

My heart sank the next day when I saw him back in the same position. He was weaker and more dishevelled than ever. He looked cold and hungry and he was shaking.

'Still here then,' I said, stroking him. 'Not looking so good today.'

This had gone on long enough. I knocked on the door of the flat.

'Sorry to bother you, mate,' I said to the unshaven guy who appeared at the door. 'Is this your cat?'

'No,' he said, looking at the ginger tom without interest. 'Nothing to do with me, mate.'

As he slammed the door, I made up my mind on the spot.

'You're coming with me,' I said.

I found the box of animal biscuits I carried specially to give treats to the cats and dogs that came up to me when I was busking. I rattled it at him and he followed me.

His back leg was injured and he was slow up the stairs. When we reached the flat, I found some milk in the fridge and mixed it with water before pouring it into a saucer. Despite what many people think, milk can be bad for cats in large amounts. He lapped it up in seconds.

I had some tuna in the fridge, so I mashed it up with some animal biscuits and gave that to him as well. Again, he wolfed it down.

Poor thing, he must be absolutely starving, I thought.

It looked like he had a nasty abscess

on his back right leg. Perhaps he'd been bitten by a dog, or a fox. He let me check his injured leg as he curled up by the radiator, and even let me sterilise the wound. Most cats would have created havoc, but he was as good as gold.

He spent the rest of the day by the radiator. But he also roamed around the flat, jumping up and scratching at whatever he could find. He had lots of pent-up energy. Young male cats who haven't been neutered can become extremely lively.

When I went to bed, he followed me into the bedroom, where he wrapped himself up into a ball by my feet. As I listened to his gentle purring in the dark, it felt good to have him there. He was company.

On Sunday morning I got up early to see if I could find his owner. There was almost always a 'Lost Cat' poster on noticeboards and bus stops. Just in case I found the owner quickly, I took the cat with me, attaching him to a lead I'd made out of a shoelace to keep him safe. He was happy to walk by my side as we went down the stairs.

Outside he began pulling on the lead. I guessed that he wanted to do his business. Sure enough he headed off into a patch of greenery to heed nature's call. He then returned to me and happily slipped back into the lead.

He must really trust me, I thought to myself. I had to repay that trust and try and help him out.

The lady across the street was known locally for looking after cats. Every cat for miles headed to her backyard knowing it was the best place to get some food. I didn't know how she could afford to feed them all.

'Isn't he lovely!' she said when she saw Bob.

'Do you recognise him?' I asked as she gave him a treat.

She shook her head. 'I've never seen him before. I bet he's come from somewhere else in London. Wouldn't surprise me if he's been dumped, poor thing.'

I had a feeling she was right about him being from somewhere else.

Back on the street, I took his lead off to see if he knew where to go. He looked at me with his big green eyes. 'I don't know where I am,' he seemed to say. 'Can't I stay with you?'

What was his story? Was he a family pet? Maybe he'd belonged to an elderly person who'd died. Or maybe he'd been a Christmas or birthday present for a family that couldn't handle him as he'd grown bigger and more boisterous. Ginger cats can be a bit bonkers and worse if not neutered.

'Enough is enough!' I imagined his previous owners saying as they dumped him on the side of the road.

Cats have a great sense of direction, but Bob hadn't tried to find his way home. Perhaps he knew that his old home was no good, and it was time to find a new owner.

The biggest clue to his identity was his

nasty injury. The wound was a few days old, and it looked like he'd got it in a fight. This suggested that he was a stray.

London has always had lots of street cats who wander the streets living off scraps and the comfort of strangers. These strays were the flotsam and jetsam of the city, fighting for survival every day. A lot of them were like this ginger tom: slightly battered, broken creatures.

Maybe he'd spotted a kindred spirit in me.

Chapter 2
Road To Recovery

When I was growing up in Australia, we had a lovely white fluffy kitten. Wherever it had come from, most probably an unlicensed pet shop, it hadn't been checked by the vet before we got it. The poor little thing was flea-ridden.

We didn't spot it at first. The kitten had such thick white fur that the fleas were festering in there and nobody knew. By the time we realised, it was too late and it died from blood loss. I was five or six at the time and was devastated. So was my mother.

I'd thought about the kitten often over the years. He was on my mind that weekend as I spent time with the ginger tom. His coat was in a terrible state. I had an awful feeling that he might suffer the same fate as the white kitten.

Sitting in the flat with him that Sunday evening, I made a decision.

'That's not going to happen to you,' I said. 'I'm taking you to a vet.'

I got up early the next morning and gave him a bowl of mashed biscuits and tuna. His leg was so bad that I knew he wouldn't be up to the ninety-minute walk, so I decided to carry him in a green recycling box. No sooner had we set off than it was clear that he didn't like it. He kept sticking his paw over the top of the box and trying to climb out. So eventually I gave up.

'Come on, I'll carry you,' I said.

He scrambled up on to my shoulders where he settled. I let him sit there while I carried the empty box with me all the way to the RSPCA centre.

The centre was packed, mostly with angry and injured dogs and their angry owners. The cat sat on my lap or on my shoulder. He was nervous, and I couldn't blame him. He was getting snarled at by most of the waiting room.

It took us four and a half hours to be seen.

'Mr Bowen?' said the nurse at last. 'The vet will see you now.'

The vet had that world-weary, seen-it-all expression you see on some people's faces.

'What seems to be the problem?' he asked me.

I told him about finding the cat in my hallway and pointed out the abscess on the back of his leg.

'I can see that he's in pain,' said the vet. 'I'll give him some painkillers and a prescription of antibiotics. Come back and see me again if things haven't improved in a fortnight.'

'Could you check him for fleas?' I asked.

The vet had a quick look around his coat but said he could find nothing. 'But it's probably worth you giving him a treatment for that. It can be a problem in young cats,' he said.

I know, I thought, remembering the white kitten.

'Let's see if he's microchipped, shall we?' said the vet.

He wasn't. Again, I wondered if he was a stray.

'Get that done when you have a chance,' the vet advised. 'He should be neutered quite soon as well. We offer a free neutering scheme for strays.'

Given the way the tom tore around the flat and was so lively with me, I nodded in agreement. 'Good idea,' I smiled.

The vet typed up his notes and printed out a prescription. Within a few minutes we were finished. Leaving the vet's surgery, I went to the dispensary and handed over the prescription.

'He's a lovely-looking fellow,' said the

white-coated lady in the dispensary. 'My mum had a ginger tom once. Best companion she ever had. Amazing temperament. Used to sit there at her feet watching the world go by. A bomb could have gone off and he wouldn't have left her. That will be twenty-two pounds please, love.'

My heart sank.

'Twenty-two pounds? Really?' I had just over thirty pounds in the whole world.

'Afraid so, love,' the nurse said.

I handed over the thirty pounds in cash and took the change. It was a lot of money for me. A day's wages. But I had no choice. I couldn't let my new friend down.

'Looks like we're stuck with each other for a while,' I said to the tom as we headed out of the door and began the long walk back to the flat. 'There's no way I'm letting you go anywhere for at least a fortnight, not until you finish your course of medicine. No one else is going to make sure you take your tablets, are they?'

I don't know why, but the responsibility of having him to look after gave me a rush of energy. I had something positive to do for someone other than myself.

I got him a supply of cat food that afternoon. It cost me around nine pounds, which really was the last money I had. That night I had to leave him on his own and head to Covent Garden with my guitar. I now had two mouths to feed.

I got to know him better over the next few days, as I nursed him back to health. By now I'd given him a name: Bob. I got the idea while watching a DVD of one of my old favourite TV series, *Twin Peaks*. There was a character in that called Killer Bob. One minute Killer Bob would be a normal, sane guy; the next he would be crazy and out of control. The tom was a bit like that. When he was happy and content he was the calmest, kindest cat you ever saw. But when the mood took him he could be an absolute maniac. So Bob it was.

It was pretty clear to me now that Bob had lived outdoors. When it came to toilet time, he absolutely refused to go in the litter tray that I'd bought for him. Instead I had to take him downstairs and let him do his business in the gardens that surrounded the flats. He'd dash off into a bit of overgrowth and do what-ever was needed, then scratch up the ground to cover up the evidence.

Our life settled into a routine. I'd leave Bob in the flat in the morning and head to Covent Garden where I'd play until I got enough cash. When I got home he'd be waiting for me at the front door. He would then follow me to the sofa in the front room and watch telly with me. When I patted the sofa and invited him to come and sit next to me, he did.

'Come on, mate,' I would coax when it was time for him to take his medicine.

'Do I have to?' he seemed to say.

But he never struggled when I put a tablet in his mouth and rubbed his throat gently until he swallowed it. Most cats go mad if you try to open their mouths. But he already trusted me.

There was something rather special about him. I'd certainly never met a cat quite like Bob.

He wasn't perfect, by any means. He regularly crashed around the kitchen, knocking over pots and pans as he searched for food. The cupboards and fridge door were covered with claw marks.

But all I had to do was say, 'No, get away from there, Bob,' and he'd slink off. It showed how intelligent he was. And again it raised all sorts of questions about his background. Would a street cat ever listen to a human? I doubted it.

I really enjoyed Bob's company, but I knew that sooner or later he would want to return to the streets. He wasn't a house cat. But for the short term I was determined to look after him as best I could.

The next morning I took Bob down to do his business outside again. He headed for the same spot in the bushes adjoining the neighbouring houses – most likely marking his territory, which cats like to do. As usual, he was in there for a minute or two then spent some time afterwards clearing up after himself.

He was making his way out when he suddenly froze, as if he'd seen something. Then he lunged forward at lightning speed. Before I knew it, Bob had grabbed at something in the grass near the hedge.

It was a little grey mouse, no more than five centimetres long.

The little fellow hadn't stood a chance.

'You're not eating that,' I said. 'Mice are full of diseases.'

I knelt down and attempted to pick it up. Bob wasn't too happy about it. He made a little noise that was part growl and part hiss. I refused to back down.

'Give it to me, Bob,' I said.

He gave me a look as if to say: 'Why should I?'

I fished around in my coat and found a nibble. 'Take this instead, Bob,' I said, offering it to him. 'It will be much better for you.'

After a few more moments, he gave in. As soon as he stepped away from the mouse, I picked it up by its tail and got rid of it.

Cats are lethal predators. A lot of people don't like to think of their cute little kitty as a mass murderer, but that's what cats are, given half a chance. In some parts of the world, they have strict rules on cats being let out at night because they destroy the local bird and rodent population.

Bob had proved it. His coolness, his speed and his skill as a killer was amazing. He knew exactly what to do and how to do it.

Before he met me, had Bob relied on finding and eating prey like this every day? Had he been raised in a home or had he always lived off the land? How had he become the cat he was today? I was sure my street cat friend had tales to tell.

In many ways, this was something else that Bob and I had in common.

Chapter 3
My Life So Far

Because I'd lived rough on the streets, people wondered about me too. How had I ended up like this?

Everyone loves to hear about how people like me fall through the cracks. I'm sure it makes them feel better about their own lives. 'Well, I may think my life is bad, but it could be worse,' they think. 'I could be that poor guy.'

People like me end up on the streets in many different ways, but there are usually some similarities. Drugs, alcohol and family problems often play a big part in the story. They certainly did for me.

I was born in Surrey, but my parents separated and my mother and I moved to Melbourne in Australia when I was three. Mum got a job working for a big photocopying company there, and was one of the company's top saleswomen.

After two years we moved to Western Australia, where we stayed until I was nine or so. Life in Australia was pretty good. I had all the space a boy could want to play in and explore the world.

The trouble was, it was very difficult to make friends at school because we moved around so much. My mother was always buying and selling houses, moving all the time. I never had a family home and never grew up in one place.

When I was nine, we moved back to the UK and to Sussex, near Horsham. I enjoyed being back in England. But then we had to move yet again – back to Western Australia, when I was about twelve.

We ended up in a place called Quinn's Rock, where a lot of my problems began. Things weren't helped by the fact that I didn't get on at all with my stepfather at the time either.

At school I was always trying too hard. I was too eager to impress, which isn't good when you are a kid. I ended up being bullied at every school I went to. I probably stuck out with my British accent and my eager-to-please attitude. I was a sitting target.

Things were particularly bad in Quinn's Rock. It was called Quinn's Rock for a reason. There were lots of nice lumps of limestone lying around wherever you looked. Perfect for throwing at a kid like me. Heading home from school one day, I was chased down the streets and stoned. At one point a stone hit me hard on the head and I got concussion.

We kept moving around throughout my early teens. It was usually connected to Mum's business ventures. Sometimes we'd have plenty of money and other times we'd have nothing. By the time I was in my mid-teens I quit school, sick to death of the bullying. I became a tearaway who was always out late, always defying Mum and thumbing my nose at authority. Predictably, I got into drugs. I was angry. I felt like I hadn't had the best breaks.

'Show me the child of seven and I'll show you the man,' they say. I'm not so sure that you'd have spotted my future when I was seven, but you could certainly have guessed what lay ahead when I was seventeen. I was on the road to self-destruction.

Mum tried her hardest to help me. She could see the damage I was doing and the problems ahead of me. She went through my pockets trying to find drugs and even locked me in my bedroom a few times. But the locks in our house were easy to pick, and I got good at picking them.

Things went from bad to worse. I was a messed-up teenager who thought he knew better than everyone. Mum must have been worried sick. I didn't care about anyone's feelings but my own.

I moved back to London to live with my half-sister from my mother's previous marriage when I was about eighteen.

Mum took me to the airport and dropped me off in the car. We were both thinking that I'd be gone for six months or so. But things didn't go to plan.

Back in the UK I couldn't get a decent job. I worked as a bartender for a while but they sacked me. My half-sister and her husband kicked me out because I wasn't much fun to live with. I met my dad a couple of times but we didn't get on. I started sleeping on friends' floors and sofas, carrying my sleeping bag around London. Then when I ran out of floors, I moved to the streets.

Things went downhill from there.

Living on the streets of London strips away everything. Your dignity, your identity. Worst of all, people see you are living on the streets and treat you as a non-person. Soon you haven't got a real friend in the world. I managed to get a job working as a kitchen porter, but they sacked me when they found out I was homeless, even though I'd done nothing wrong at work.

The one thing that might have saved me was going back to Australia. I had a return ticket but lost my passport two weeks before the flight. Any hope of getting back to my family in Australia disappeared. And in a way, so did I.

The next phase of my life was a fog of drugs, drink, petty crime and hopeless-ness.

By 1998 I was totally dependent on heroin. I probably came close to death a few times. During that period I never thought of contacting my family. I can only imagine what they must have gone through.

After about a year of this, I was picked up off the streets by a homeless charity and stayed in various shelters. For the best part of the next decade I ended up living in horrendous hostels, B&Bs and houses, sharing my space with drug addicts who stole everything I owned. I slept with my most important possessions tucked inside my clothes. It was all about survival.

My drug use got so bad that I ended up on a drug rehabilitation programme. I did some counselling there, where I talked about my habit, how it had started and how I was going to bring it to an end.

I had become addicted to heroin because I was lonely, pure and simple. I was on my own and, strange though it sounds, it felt like heroin was my only friend. But deep down, I knew it was killing me.

I slowly moved off heroin on to methadone, which is the first step in escaping addiction. By the spring of 2007, I planned to stop taking methadone as well, and get off drugs completely.

The move to my flat in Tottenham, in an ordinary apartment block full of ordinary families, gave me the opportunity to get my life back on track. To pay the rent, I started busking in Covent Garden. It wasn't much, but it helped put food on the table and pay the bills. This was my chance to turn the corner. I had to take it.

If I'd been a cat, I'd have been on my ninth life.

Chapter 4
The Snip

By the end of Bob's second week of medication, he was looking a lot brighter. The wound at the back of his leg was healing nicely. The bald patches on his coat began to disappear and were replaced with new, thicker fur. He also seemed happier in his face. There was a beautiful, green and yellow glow to his eyes that hadn't been there before.

His boisterousness around the flat proved that he was feeling better. He had flown around the place since day one, but in the past week or so he'd become even more of a ball of energy. There were times when he jumped and ran around the place like a maniac. He clawed furiously at everything and anything he could find, including me. I didn't mind. He was only playing.

He became such a menace in the kitchen that I had to buy a couple of cheap plastic child-locks to protect my food. I also had to be careful about leaving anything lying around that he might play with. A pair of shoes or item of clothing could be scratched to bits within minutes.

There was no doubt in my mind that Bob needed neutering.

If I didn't have him neutered, his hormones would completely take over. He would probably go missing for days or weeks at a time, looking for females. He'd be far more likely to get run over and to get into fights. There was also a small risk of him contracting some nasty diseases. If I neutered him, he would be much calmer and more even-tempered. It was a no-brainer.

A couple of days before he finished his tablets, I called the local clinic.

'Is my cat eligible for a free neutering operation?' I asked.

'Yes,' the nurse told me. 'Does he have a certificate from a vet?'

I said that I'd got a certificate after my visit to the RSPCA vet for Bob's leg and his flea and worm tablets. That was fine, she said.

'What about the medication that he's on?' I asked. 'He's finishing a course of antibiotics.'

'That shouldn't be a problem,' she assured me. 'We can book him in for an operation in two days' time.'

I got up nice and early on the day of the operation. We had to be at the surgery by 10am. I stuck Bob in the same green, plastic recycling box I'd used a fortnight earlier to take him to the RSPCA. The weather was miserable, so I rested the lid loosely on the box once we were out and about. He didn't like it any more than he had the first time I put him in it. He kept sticking his head out and watching the world go by.

We got to the clinic in plenty of time for his appointment. It was the usual chaotic scene, with dogs tugging on their owners' leashes and growling at the cats inside their carriers. Bob stood out like a sore thumb in his green box, but he wasn't fazed at all. He seemed to have placed his trust in me.

'Mr Bowen?' said a young nurse. 'Follow me, please.'

We went into a room, where she asked me a few questions.

'The operation can't be reversed,' she warned me. 'Are you certain you don't want to breed from Bob?'

'Yeah, I'm quite certain,' I said, rubbing Bob on the head.

'And how old is Bob?'

'I don't know,' I confessed, and explained Bob's story.

'Hmm, let's take a look.' The nurse examined Bob. 'If male cats aren't neutered, they change their appearance as they mature,' she explained. 'They get fuller faces, particularly around the cheeks. They also develop thicker skins and generally become quite big. Bob's not that big, so I'd guess that he's maybe nine to ten months old.'

Bob was practically a kitten!

'There's a tiny risk of complications,' she said as she passed me some forms to fill in. 'But we will give him a thorough examination and maybe run a blood test before we do the operation. If there's a problem we will contact you.'

'OK,' I said, feeling sheepish. I didn't have a mobile phone, so they would have trouble contacting me.

The nurse explained what the operation would entail.

'If everything goes OK, you can come and collect Bob in six hours,' she said, looking down at her watch. 'So at around four-thirty. Is that OK?'

After giving Bob a final cuddle, I headed back out into the overcast streets. I didn't have time to go all the way into central London for my usual busking. So I decided to take my chances around the nearest railway station, Dalston Kingsland. I earned a few quid and whiled away the hours as I waited for Bob, and there was a friendly cobbler's shop next to the station where I got shelter from the rain when it came.

I tried to block Bob out of my thoughts as I played my guitar. I'd heard stories of cats and dogs going into vets' surgeries for the most minor procedures and never coming out again. I struggled to keep my darkest thoughts at bay. It didn't help that there were big black clouds glowering over me.

Time passed very, very slowly. At last the clock reached 4.15pm and I began packing up. I almost ran the last few hundred yards to the clinic.

The nurse I'd seen earlier was at the reception desk. She greeted me with a warm smile.

'How is he? Did it all go all right?' I asked, still breathing heavily.

It was weird. I hadn't felt this concerned about someone – or some-thing – for years.

'He's absolutely fine. Don't worry,' she said. 'Get your breath back and I'll take you through.'

I went into the surgical area and saw Bob lying in a nice warm cage.

'Hello, Bob mate, how you doing?' I said, awash with relief.

He was still very dopey and drowsy so didn't recognise me for a while, but when he did he sat up and started clawing at the doors of the cage.

'Let me outta here!' he seemed to say.

I signed some papers as the nurse checked Bob one last time to make sure he was fit to leave. She was really lovely and very helpful.

'If you notice any problems then give us a ring or bring him back in so we can check him out. But I'm sure he'll be fine,' she told me.

'How long will he be groggy?' I asked.

'It varies a lot,' she said. 'Some cats bounce back immediately. Others take longer. But they are normally as right as rain within forty-eight hours. He probably won't want to eat much tomorrow, but his appetite will return fairly soon. But like I say, call us if you're worried about anything.'

I was about to put Bob back in the recycling box when she stopped me.

'I think we can do better than that,' she said, and produced a lovely, sky-blue carrying case.

'Oh, that's not mine,' I said.

'It's OK,' she promised. 'We've got loads of spares, you can have this one. Just drop it back in when you're next passing.'

'Really?'

How could such a good carrying case be going spare? Maybe someone had left it behind. Or maybe someone had brought their cat in and returned to discover that it would not be needed any more. I didn't want to think about that too much.

I took the day off work the next day to make sure Bob was OK. He was supposed to be supervised for twenty-four to forty-eight hours after the operation, to make sure there weren't any side effects. Although I needed the money, I could never have forgiven myself if something had gone wrong. So I stayed in the flat on twenty-four-hour Bob watch.

The next morning, Bob ate a little breakfast, which was encouraging. He also wandered around the flat a little bit, although he wasn't his normal bouncy self.

Over the next couple of days, he became more like the old Bob. Soon he was wolfing down his food just like before. He was still in a bit of pain, but it wasn't a major problem.

I was glad I'd acted.

Chapter 5
Ticket To Ride

It was time to get Bob out of the flat and back on to the streets where he belonged. I guessed that he would want to get back to his old life now that he was well again and fully recovered from his operation.

I took him downstairs.

'Off you go then, mate,' I said, and pointed in the direction of the street.

Bob looked confused.

'What do you want me to do?' he seemed to say.

'Go, go, go on,' I said, making sweeping movements with my hands.

He padded off towards the patch of ground where he liked to do his business. When he was finished, he strolled back towards me. This time his expression said: 'OK, I did what you wanted. What now?'

For the first time, a thought popped into my head.

'I think you want to hang around,' I said.

Part of me was pleased, but I knew I shouldn't let it happen. I was still struggling to look after myself. How was I meant to look after a cat as well? It wasn't fair on either of us.

So, with a heavy heart, I decided that

when I went to work in the morning, I would take him out of the flat and leave him outside in the gardens.

'Tough love,' I told myself.

He didn't like it one bit.

The first time I did it, he shot me a look of disgust.

'Traitor,' he seemed to say.

As I headed off with my guitar, he followed, zigzagging across the pavement like some spy as he tried to remain unseen. Except it was easy to spot his distinctive ginger fur, bobbing and weaving around.

Each time I saw him, I stopped.

'Oh mate. Please. Go away!' I begged, flamboyantly waving at him until he got the message and disappeared.

When I got back six hours later, he was waiting for me at the entrance to the flats.

Part of me wanted to stop him coming in. But that part was overwhelmed by the one that was touched by the loyalty he was showing, and wanted to invite him up to the flat to curl up at my feet.

We settled into a bit of a routine.

Each day I left him outside, and each night when I got back from busking, he was waiting for me. It was obvious he wasn't going away.

I had to take the ultimate step and leave him out overnight.

The first night I did it, I tried to sneak in without him seeing me. Stupid move. He had more senses in one of his whiskers than I had in my entire body. No sooner had I opened the door to the building than he was there, squeezing his way in. Even though it pained me, I left him outside in the hallway that night, but he was waiting on my doormat in the morning.

For the next few days we went through the same performance. He always won.

Then he started following me again.

The first time he came as far as the main road. The next time he tailed me for a hundred yards towards my bus stop. A part of me admired his determination, but another part of me was cursing him. Each day he grew bolder and bolder. And each night I got home, there he was – waiting.

Something had to give eventually. And it did.

One day I headed out for work as usual. I saw Bob sitting in an alleyway.

'Hi mate,' I said.

He started following me, but I shooed him away as usual and he slunk off.

There was no sign of him as I went down the road.

Perhaps he's finally got the message, I thought to myself.

To get to my bus stop, I had to cross Tottenham High Road, one of the busiest and most dangerous roads in north London. As I stood on the pavement, trying to cross through the busy traffic, I felt something rub against my leg. I looked down.

'Bob!' I gasped.

To my horror, Bob was beside me, trying to cross the road as well.

'What are you doing here?' I hissed at him.

He looked at me. 'Stupid question,' he seemed to say.

I couldn't let him risk it. So I swept him up and put him on my shoulder, where I knew he liked to sit. He sat there, snuggled up against the side of my head, as I crossed the road.

'All right, Bob, that's far enough,' I said to him as I put him down on the pavement.

He sidled off down the street into the throng.

Maybe now I've seen the last of him, I thought to myself.

A few moments later the bus pulled up. It was an old-fashioned red double-decker Routemaster bus that you could jump on at the back. I went to sit on the bench at the back of the bus when, behind me, I saw a sudden flash of ginger fur.

Before I knew it, Bob had jumped up and plonked himself on the seat next to

me. I was gobsmacked. I realised –
finally – that I wasn't ever going to shake
this cat off.

'OK,' I laughed, and patted my lap.
'On you get.'

Bob jumped on to my lap at once. A
moment or two later, the conductor
appeared. She was a cheerful West
Indian lady and smiled at Bob, then me.

'Is he yours?' she said, stroking him.

'I guess he must be,' I said.

For the next forty-five minutes, Bob sat
next to me, his face pressed against the
glass of the bus window, watching the
world go by. He seemed fascinated by all
the cars, cyclists, vans and pedestrians
whizzing past. He wasn't fazed at all.

The only time he pulled away from the window and looked to me for reassurance was when the blare of a police siren, a fire engine or an ambulance took him by surprise or got a bit too close for comfort.

'Nothing to worry about,' I told him, each time giving him a friendly stroke on the back of the neck. 'This is what the middle of London sounds like, Bob. You'd better get used to it.'

Somehow I knew this wouldn't be the last time we'd make this trip together. I had a feeling that he was here in my life to stay.

Chapter 6
Centre of Attention

We got off at my usual bus stop near Tottenham Court Road tube station. On the pavement, I fished around in my coat pocket and found the makeshift shoelace lead. I put it around Bob's neck. I didn't want him wandering off. He'd be lost in a second – or, even worse, crushed by one of the buses or black cabs whistling towards and from Oxford Street.

Understandably, it was all a bit scary for Bob. As we picked our way through the throngs of tourists and shoppers, I could tell that he was uneasy. So I decided to take one of my short cuts through the back streets to get to Covent Garden.

'Come on, Bob, let's get you out of the crowds,' I said.

Even then he wasn't happy. After only a few yards I could tell that he wanted me to pick him up.

'All right, but don't make a habit of it,' I said, gathering him up and placing him on my shoulders just as I'd done crossing Tottenham High Road.

He soon settled into a comfortable spot, looking out like he was in the crow's-nest on a pirate ship. I probably looked like Long John Silver, but with a puss rather than a parrot. I could feel him purring lightly as we walked down towards Covent Garden.

After a while I began to forget Bob was there. Instead I started thinking my usual thoughts. Was the weather going to be good enough for five hours' busking? What sort of crowd would there be in Covent Garden? How long would it take me to make the twenty or thirty pounds I needed to get me – and now Bob – through the next few days? It had taken me nearly five hours the previous day.

I was mulling these things over when I suddenly became aware of something.

Ordinarily, no one even glanced at me. I was a busker and this was London. I didn't exist. I was a person to be avoided. But as I walked down Neal Street that afternoon, almost every person we passed was looking at me. Well, more to the point, they were look- ing at Bob.

One or two had confused looks on their faces. It must have looked weird, a tall, long-haired bloke walking along with a large, ginger tom on his shoulders. Not something you see every day – even on the streets of London. But most people broke into broad smiles. It wasn't long before people were stopping us.

'Ah, look at you two,' said one well- dressed, middle-aged lady laden down with shopping bags. 'He's gorgeous. Can I stroke him?'

'Of course,' I said, thinking it would be a one-off event.

She plonked down her bags and placed her face right up to his.

'What a lovely fellow you are, aren't

you?' she said. 'Isn't he good to sit there on your shoulders like that? Don't see that very often. He must really trust you.'

I'd barely said goodbye to the lady when we were approached by two Swedish teenagers on holiday.

'What is his name? Can we take his picture?' they said, snapping away with their cameras the instant I nodded.

'His name's Bob,' I said.

'Ah, Bob. Cool.'

I had to politely excuse myself after a couple of minutes. We carried on towards the bottom of Neal Street in the direction of Long Acre. But the going was slow. I'd barely go a metre without being stopped by someone who wanted to stroke or talk to Bob. It was ridiculous.

It normally took me around ten

minutes to get from my bus stop to my busking pitch. But by the time we got to Covent Garden it was almost an hour after I normally got set up.

Thanks a lot, Bob, you've probably cost me a few quid in lost earnings, I thought. I was only half joking. If he was going to slow me down this much every day, I really couldn't let him follow me on to the bus again.

It wasn't long before I was thinking a bit differently.

By this point, I'd been busking around Covent Garden for about a year and a half. I started at about two or three in the afternoon and carried on until around eight in the evening. At the weekends I would go earlier and do lunchtimes. On Thursday, Friday and Saturday I'd carry on until quite late, trying to take advantage of the extra numbers of Londoners that hung around at the end of the working week.

For the last couple of hours each day I'd walk around all the pubs in Covent Garden where people were standing outside. In the summer months this could be productive, but also risky. Some people didn't like me approaching them and could be rude and even abusive. But I was used to that. There were plenty of people who were happy to hear me play a song then slip me a quid.

Street entertainers were meant to work in different parts of Covent Garden. Musicians played near the Royal Opera House and Bow Street, while the jugglers and other street entertainers worked on the west side of the piazza. James Street was for the human statues, but it was normally clear so I had made it my own little pitch. There was always the risk of getting moved to Bow Street with the other musicians, but it was worth it. The number of people coming out of the tube station there was huge. If only one in a thousand gave me some money, then I could do OK.

Arriving at my pitch, I checked to make sure the coast was clear. No one official seemed to be around. So I put Bob down on the pavement near the wall, unzipped my guitar case, took off my jacket and got ready to tune up.

A couple of people slowed down in front of me and lobbed coins into my guitar case even before I'd played a note. *Generous of them*, I thought.

Behind me I heard a male voice. 'Nice cat, mate,' he said.

I turned and saw an ordinary-looking guy in his mid-twenties giving me a thumbs up sign and walking off with a smile on his face.

I was taken aback. Bob had curled himself up in a comfortable ball in the middle of the empty guitar case. I knew he was a charmer. But this was something else.

Chapter 7
Teamwork

I'd taught myself to play the guitar
when I was a teenager living back in
Australia. People would show me things
and then I'd work my way through
them on my own. I got my first guitar
when I was fifteen or sixteen. It was
quite late to start playing, I suppose. I
loved Jimi Hendrix, and had wanted to
play like him.

The set I busked with was full of the music I loved: Nirvana, Bob Dylan and a fair bit of Johnny Cash. The most popular song in my set was 'Wonderwall' by Oasis. That always worked best, especially outside the pubs when I wandered around later in the evenings.

I'd barely been playing for more than a few minutes when a group of kids stopped. They were all wearing Brazilian football shirts and speaking what I recognised as Portuguese. One of them, a young girl, bent down and began stroking Bob.

'Ah, *gato bonito*,' she said.

'She is saying you have a beautiful cat,' one of the boys translated.

Almost immediately other people were stopping to see what the fuss was about. About half a dozen of the Brazilian kids and other passers-by began fishing around in their pockets and started raining coins into the bag.

'Looks like you may not be such a bad companion after all, Bob. I'll invite you out for the day more often,' I smiled at him.

I'd not planned on bringing him along with me so I didn't have much to give him. There was a half-empty packet of his favourite cat treats in my rucksack so I gave him one of them every now and again. Like me, he'd have to wait until later to get a decent meal.

As the late afternoon turned into the early evening and the crowds thickened with people heading home from work or out into the West End for the evening, more and more people were slowing down and looking at Bob.

As darkness started to fall, one middle-aged lady stopped for a chat.

'How long have you had him?' she asked, bending down to stroke Bob.

'Oh, only a few weeks,' I said. 'We sort of found each other.'

'Found each other? Sounds interesting.'

She smiled as I explained the story of how we'd met and how I'd spent a fortnight nursing him back to health.

'I had a ginger tom very much like this one a few years ago,' she said. For a moment I thought she was going to burst into tears. 'You are lucky to have found him. They are just the best companions, they are so quiet and docile. You've found yourself a real friend there.'

'I think you are right,' I smiled.

She placed a fiver into the guitar case before leaving.

After just over an hour, I had as much as I'd normally make in a good day: just over twenty pounds.

This is brilliant, I thought to myself.

But something inside me was saying that I shouldn't call it quits just yet.

I was a bit torn about Bob. Despite my gut feeling that this cat and I were somehow destined to be together, I still figured that he'd eventually go off and make his own way. So as the passers-by continued to slow down and make a fuss of him, I figured I might as well make the most of it. Make hay while the sun shines and all that.

'If he wants to come out and have fun with me, that's great,' I said to myself. 'And if I'm making a bit of cash as well, then that's great too.'

Except that it was more than just a bit of cash by now.

I had been used to making around twenty pounds a day. But that night, it was clear that I'd made a lot more than that.

After packing up my guitar, I totted it all up. I had made the princely sum of £63.77. To most of the people walking around Covent Garden that might not have seemed like a lot of money. But it was to me.

I transferred all the coins into my rucksack and hauled it on to my shoulders. It was rattling like a giant piggy bank. It also weighed a ton! I was ecstatic. That was the most I'd ever made in a day's work on the streets.

I picked up Bob, giving him a stroke on the back of the neck.

'Well done, mate,' I said. 'That was what I call a good day's work.'

I decided that I didn't need to wander around the pubs tonight. Bob was hungry – as was I. We needed to head home.

I walked back towards Tottenham Court Road and the bus stop with Bob on my shoulder once again. I decided not to talk to absolutely everyone who stopped and smiled at us. I couldn't. There were too many of them. I wanted to get home this side of midnight.

'We'll have something nice to eat tonight, Bob,' I said as we settled on to the bus for the trip home.

Bob pinned his nose up against the window, watching the bright lights and the traffic.

We got off the bus near a really nice Indian restaurant on Tottenham High Road. I'd never had enough spare money to be able to afford anything on its delicious menu. But that night I went in.

'A chicken tikka masala with lemon rice, a peshwari naan and a sag paneer, please mate,' I said.

The waiters threw me a few funny looks when they saw Bob on a lead beside me.

'I'll pop back in twenty minutes to collect it,' I said, and headed off with Bob to a supermarket across the road.

'How about a nice pouch of posh cat food, Bob?' I suggested in the supermarket. 'And a couple of packs of your favourite nibbles and some special cat milk? Let's push the boat out. It's been a day to remember.'

After picking up our dinner, I almost ran home, I was so overwhelmed by the tempting smells coming out from the brown paper carrier bag from the curry house. When we got inside Bob and I both wolfed down our food as if there was no tomorrow. I hadn't eaten so well in months, maybe years. I'm pretty sure Bob hadn't either.

We then curled up for a couple of hours, me watching television and him snuggled up in his favourite spot under the radiator. We both slept like logs that night.

Chapter 8
One Man and His Cat

The next morning I was woken by a loud clanging noise coming from the kitchen. It sounded like Bob was trying to open the cupboards where I kept his food and had knocked something over. It was his way of saying: 'Get up, I want my breakfast.'

I hauled myself out of bed and stumbled into the kitchen.

'OK, mate, I get the picture,' I yawned, unlocking the cupboards and reaching for a sachet of his favourite chicken dish.

He devoured it in seconds. He then gulped down the water in his bowl, licked his face and paws clean and trotted off into the living room, where he took up his favourite position under the radiator.

If only all our lives were that simple, I thought to myself.

I'd considered not going to work, but then thought better of it. We may have had a lucky break last night, but that money wouldn't keep us going for long. I had a new responsibility in my life and an extra mouth to feed – a rather hungry one.

I wasn't sure whether Bob would want to come out busking with me again today. But I put some snacks in the bag for him just in case he did decide to follow me again.

It was early afternoon as I headed off with my rucksack and guitar lashed across my back. As I was about to shut the door behind me, Bob bolted towards me and followed me out into the corridor and towards the staircase.

On the ground floor he did his business in the bushes and then trotted off towards the area where the bins were kept.

He was fascinated by the bins. Goodness knows what he was finding – and eating – in there. I wasn't too happy about it. Luckily there must have been a collection earlier that morning because there was no stray rubbish around.

I decided to head off without him. I

knew he'd get back inside the building somehow, and would probably be waiting on the landing for me when I got home that evening.

Fair enough, I thought. Bob had done me a huge favour the previous day. I wasn't going to exploit him by demanding he come along with me every day. He was my companion, not my employee!

The skies were grey and there was a hint of rain in the air. Busking on a rainy day was never a good idea. Instead of feeling sympathy for you, people simply rushed by that bit quicker. If it was bucketing down in the centre of town, I decided I'd head back to spend the day hanging out with Bob.

I was about two hundred yards or so down the road when I sensed something behind me. I turned round and saw a familiar figure, padding along the pavement.

'Ah, changed our mind have we?' I said.

Bob gave me a pitying look, as if to say: 'Well, why else would I be standing here?'

I still had the shoelace lead in my pocket. I put it on him and we started walking down the road together.

People immediately began staring at us. One or two looked at me disapprovingly. They clearly thought I was off my rocker, leading a ginger tom around on a shoelace.

'If this is going to become a regular thing I really am going to have to get you a proper lead,' I said quietly to Bob, suddenly feeling a bit self-conscious.

But for every person that gave me a

dirty look, another half dozen smiled and nodded at me. One African lady, weighed down with bags of shopping, gave us a big, sunny grin.

'Don't you two make a pretty picture,' she said.

No one had talked to me on the streets around my flat in all the months I'd lived there. It was odd, but also amazing. It was as if my Harry Potter invisibility cloak had slipped off my shoulders.

When we got to the crossing point at Tottenham High Road, Bob looked at me.

'Come on, you know what to do now,' he seemed to be saying.

So I plonked him on my shoulder, crossed the road and caught the bus.

I'd been right about the weather. The rain started hammering down, making patterns on the bus window where Bob once more pressed his face tight against the glass. Outside you could just make out a sea of umbrellas. There were people running, splashing through the streets to avoid the downpour.

Thankfully, the rain had eased off by the time we reached the centre of town. Despite the weather, there were even bigger crowds than there had been the previous day.

'We'll give it a go for a couple of hours,' I said to Bob as I put him on my shoulder and headed off towards Covent Garden. 'But if it starts to rain again we'll head back, I promise.'

Walking down Neal Street, once again people were stopping us all the time. I was happy to let them fuss over Bob, within reason. But I quickly learned to keep moving, otherwise I was surrounded before I knew it.

It was as we were reaching the end of Neal Street near where I turned towards James Street that something interesting happened.

I suddenly felt Bob readjusting his paws on my shoulder. Before I knew it he was sliding off my shoulder and clambering down my arm. When I let him hop on to the pavement he began walking ahead of me on his lead. He recognised where we were and he was leading the way.

He marched ahead of me all the way to the pitch where we'd been the previous night. He then stood there, waiting for me to take out my guitar and lay the case down for him.

'There you go, Bob,' I said.

He instantly sat down on the soft case as if it was where he belonged. He positioned himself so that he could watch the world walk by. In Covent Garden, it really does.

Chapter 9
In the Money

There had been a time when I'd had ambitions of making it as a real musician like Kurt Cobain. As stupid as it sounds now, it had been part of my grand plan when I'd come back to England from Australia.

That's what I'd told my mother and everyone else when I'd set off.

For a brief time, I felt like I might

actually get somewhere. It was hard for a while, but in 2002 I got together with some guys I'd met. We formed a four-piece guitar band called HyperFury. The name certainly summed me up. I really was hyper-furious, and my music was an outlet for my anger and angst.

Our songs were edgy and dark and so were our lyrics. But put it this way: we didn't get booked for Glastonbury.

We did have some fans, though, and managed to get some gigs. There was a big Gothic kind of scene going on in north London and we fitted in well with it. We played wherever we were invited. The biggest gig we did was at The Dublin Castle, a famous music pub in north London, where we played a couple of times.

Things were going so well for us at one point that a mate and I teamed up and started our own independent label, Corrupt Drive Records. But it didn't really work. Or, to be more accurate, I didn't really work.

By 2005 I'd accepted that the band was a hobby, not a way of making a living. I was struggling so badly with my drug habit that I fell by the wayside – again. It became another one of those second chances that I let slip through my fingers. I guess I'll never know what might have been.

I'd never given up on music, however. Even when the band broke up, I would spend hours most days playing on the guitar, improvising songs. I don't know where I'd have been without it. And the money I made at busking had certainly made a difference to my life in recent years.

That evening was a repeat of the previous day. The moment I sat down – or, more precisely, the moment Bob sat down - people who would normally have rushed by began to slow down and interact with him.

Not long after I'd started playing, a stony-faced traffic warden walked past. She looked down at Bob and her face melted into a warm smile.

'Aah, look at you,' she said, stopping and kneeling down to stroke Bob.

She barely gave me a second glance and didn't drop anything into the guitar case. But that was fine. I was beginning to love the way that Bob could brighten up people's days.

He was a beautiful creature, there was no doubt about that. But it wasn't just that. There was something else about Bob. It was his personality that was attracting their attention. People could sense something special about him.

I could sense it myself. He had an unusual rapport with people – or at least, people he knew had his best interests at heart.

Every now and again I'd see him bridle a bit when he saw someone he didn't like. At one point a very smart, rich-looking Middle-Eastern guy walked past, arm in arm with a really attractive blond woman.

'Oh, look. What a gorgeous cat,' she said, pulling on the guy's arm to slow him down.

The guy flicked his hand dismissively, as if to say, 'So what?'

The instant he did so Bob's body language changed. He arched his back ever so slightly and shifted his body position so that he was a few inches closer to me. It was subtle – but to me it was really telling.

I wonder whether this guy reminds Bob of someone from his past? I thought to myself as the couple walked on.

I'd have given anything to know Bob's story, but it was something I was never going to find out. It would always be guesswork.

The way Bob had sucked in the audience the previous day had been a bit odd for me. But I felt relaxed that day as I settled into my set. That day I felt like we were safe, like we belonged there.

As I began singing and the coins started tinkling into the case, I thought to myself: *I'm enjoying this.*

It had been a long time since I'd said that.

By the time we headed home three hours later my rucksack was once more jangling with the weight of coins. We'd collected well over sixty pounds again.

This time I wasn't going to spend it on an expensive curry. I had more practical uses for the money in mind.

Chapter 10
Days Off

The following day the weather was even worse. So I decided to spend some time on Bob rather than busking. If he was going to hang out with me on a regular basis then he needed better equipment. I couldn't walk around with him attached to a leash made out of a shoelace. Apart from anything else, it was uncomfortable and dangerous.

Bob and I hopped on a bus and headed off in the direction of Archway. The north London branch of the Cats Protection charity was there.

Bob sensed immediately that this wasn't the same route we'd taken the previous couple of days. Every now and again he would turn and look at me.

'Where are you taking me today?' he seemed to say.

He wasn't anxious, just curious.

The Cats Protection shop had all sorts of equipment, toys and books about cats.

'He's a good-looking boy isn't he?' said one of the two ladies working there. Bob leaned his body into her as she smoothed his coat and cooed over him.

'He wandered into my block of flats,' I explained. 'And he's been following me around ever since. Even on the bus!'

'A lot of cats like to go out with their owners,' one of the ladies told me. 'They like to go for a walk in the park or for a short stroll down the street. But I have to say Bob's a bit unusual, isn't he?'

'He is,' said the other lady. 'You've got yourself a jewel there. He's obviously decided to attach himself to you.'

Every now and again, I wondered whether I should try harder to put Bob back on the streets, and whether I was doing the right thing in keeping him in the flat with me. The words of the Cats Protection ladies were a real boost.

But I didn't know how to look after Bob properly if he was going to be my constant companion on the streets of London. There were all sorts of potential threats and dangers out there.

'The best thing you can do is to get a

harness like this,' one of the ladies said, unhooking a nice-looking blue, woven nylon harness, collar and matching lead. 'It's not a great idea just to fix a leash to a cat collar. The worst collars can harm your cat's neck and even choke the cat. And the problem with the better quality collars is that they are made from elastic, or are what they call 'breakaway' collars, so that the cat can escape if the collar gets caught on something. There's a good chance that at some point you'll have an empty leash dangling in your hand.'

I certainly didn't want that to happen in the middle of London.

'I think you would be much better off with a cat harness and a leash, especially if you are out with Bob all the time,' the lady said.

'Isn't it going to feel funny for him?' I asked.

'You'll need to ease him into it,' she agreed. 'It might take a week or so. Start him off wearing it for a few minutes a day before you are ready to go outside together. Then build it up from there.'

The harness, collar and leash cost about thirteen pounds. It was one of the most expensive they had, but I figured he was worth it.

I began just by letting Bob wear it around the house, sometimes with the lead attached. At first he was a bit confused at having this extra-long woven nylon tail trailing behind him. But he soon got used to it.

'Well done, mate,' I said every time he wore it. Praising him was really important.

After a couple of days we started going on short walks with it. Slowly but surely it became second nature to him to have the harness on.

Bob was still coming with me every day.

We never stayed out too long. Even though I had a feeling he would follow me to the ends of the earth, and even though he was always sitting on my shoulders and didn't have to walk, I wasn't going to do that to him.

It was during the third week of us busking together that he first decided he didn't want to join me. As I went through the normal routine, he just shuffled off behind the sofa for a bit, then went and lay down underneath the radiator.

He was basically saying: 'I'm having a day off.'

I could tell he was tired.

'Don't fancy it today, Bob?' I said, stroking him.

He looked at me in that knowing way of his.

'No problem,' I said.

I put some snacks in a bowl to keep him going for the rest of the day. I'd heard that putting the TV on made pets feel less lonely when their owners were out. I didn't know whether that was true, but I switched the TV set on in any case. He immediately shuffled towards his favourite spot and started staring at it.

Going out that day really brought home the difference Bob had made to my life. When he was with me, I turned heads everywhere. On my own I was invisible again.

By now we were well known enough to the locals for a few people to express concern.

'Where's the cat today?' one local stall-owner said as he passed me by that evening.

'He's having a day off,' I said.

'Oh, good. I was worried something had happened to the little fella,' he smiled, giving me the thumbs-up.

A couple of other people stopped and asked the same question. As soon as I'd told them Bob was fine, they moved on. No one was quite as interested in stopping for a talk as they were when Bob was around. I may not have liked it, but I accepted it. That's the way it was.

As I played on the pavement at James

Street, I also noticed that I wasn't making anywhere near as much money. It took me a few more hours to earn about half the cash I had made on a good day with Bob. But that was OK.

It was as I walked back that evening that something began to sink in. It wasn't all about making money. I wasn't going to starve. And my life was much richer for having Bob in it. It was such a pleasure to have such great company, such a wonderful companion. This was my chance to get back on track.

On the streets, people don't want to give you a chance. All they see is someone they think is trying to get a free ride. When I approach them, they don't understand I'm working, not begging. Just because I don't wear a suit and a tie and carry a briefcase or a computer, it doesn't mean that I'm freeloading.

Having Bob with me gave me a chance to interact with people.

They would ask where Bob came from and I'd explain how we got together and how we were making money to pay our rent, food, electricity and gas bills. People would give me more of a fair hearing and begin to see me in a different light.

Cats are notoriously picky about who they like. And if a cat doesn't like its owner, it will go and find another one. Cats do that all the time. Seeing me with my cat softened me in people's eyes. It humanised me. Especially after I'd been so dehumanised. In some ways it was giving me back my identity.

I had been a non-person. Now at last I was becoming a person again.

Chapter 11
The Two Musketeers

Being responsible for someone other than myself had come as a bit of a shock. But I enjoyed it. Bob was my baby and making sure he was warm, well fed and safe was really rewarding.

But it was scary too. I worried about him all the time, especially when we were out on the streets. And with good cause.

The streets of London weren't all filled with kind-hearted tourists and cat lovers. I still got abuse when I was busking, usually from drunken young blokes showing off to their mates.

'Do a proper day's work, you long-haired layabout!' they would shout.

I let their insults wash over me. I was used to them. But my protective instincts really took over when they turned on Bob.

One Friday evening, I was busking in James Street when a bunch of rowdy young lads came past, on the lookout for trouble. A couple of them spotted Bob sitting on the pavement next to me and started teasing him, shouting: 'Woof! Meow!' Their mates thought it was hilarious.

Then one of them kicked the guitar

case with Bob sitting in it. It sent the case – and Bob – sliding a foot or so along the pavement.

Bob was really distressed. He made a loud noise, almost like a scream, and jumped out of the case. Thankfully his lead was attached, or otherwise he would almost certainly have run off into the crowds. He hid behind my rucksack instead.

I got up immediately and confronted the guy.

'What did you do that for?' I demanded. I'm quite tall and towered over him, but it didn't seem to faze him.

'I just wanted to see if the cat was real,' he laughed.

I didn't see the funny side of it.

'That's really clever,' I said.

They all began circling me and one of

them began shoving into me with his chest and shoulders. I stood my ground and shoved him back.

'Go on then, do what you want,' I challenged, pointing to a CCTV camera on the corner near us. 'You're on camera.'

Their faces were a picture. They knew you couldn't get away with violence on camera. They moved on, waving their arms and making every offensive gesture known to man. Sticks and stones and all that. I wasn't worried. In fact, I felt good about seeing them off. But I didn't hang around much longer that evening. I knew their type. They didn't take kindly to being 'dissed'.

The incident proved a couple of things. First, it was always a good idea to be near a CCTV camera. Second, I really was on my own when trouble flared like this. There wasn't a policeman in sight, nor any assistance from the staff in the tube station. A lot of people were milling around when the gang confronted me, but no one helped me. Most of them did their best to melt into the background and shuffle off. Nobody was going to help a long-haired busker and his cat.

'It's you and me against the world, Bob,' I said to him as we headed home on the bus. 'We're the two Musketeers.'

Bob nuzzled up to me and purred lightly, as if in agreement.

It wasn't just people we had to worry about. There were a lot of dogs on the streets of London too. It was no surprise that many of them took an instant interest in Bob. Fortunately Bob didn't seem too bothered. He just ignored them. If they came up to him he would just stare them out.

I found out just how well Bob could handle himself against a dog a week or so after the incident with the gang.

We were sitting in Neal Street in the late afternoon when a guy with a Staffordshire Bull Terrier loomed into view. The Staffie spotted Bob and instantly started straining at his leash.

He was just checking Bob out – or rather, checking out the biscuits Bob had in front of him. He started inching his way towards the bowl, sniffing excitedly at the prospect of a free titbit or two.

I couldn't believe what happened next.

Bob had been snoozing peacefully at

my side. But as the Staffie leaned in towards the biscuits, he calmly picked himself up and then just bopped the dog on the nose with his paw. It was so lightning fast it was a punch to do Muhammad Ali proud.

The dog couldn't believe it. He just jumped back in shock. I was almost as shocked as the dog, I think, and laughed out loud.

The owner gave the dog a whack around the head, then tugged on its lead to move on. I think he was embarrassed that a cat had made his fearsome dog look stupid.

Bob went back to snoozing at my feet, as if bopping a ferocious dog on the nose was like swatting a pesky fly. It was a really revealing moment. Bob clearly wasn't afraid to defend himself. In fact, he knew how to look after himself rather well. Where had he learned to do that?

Once more I was fascinated by the same old questions. Where had he grown up? What adventures had he had before he had joined up with me and become the second Musketeer?

Chapter 12
Bob's Quirks

Living with Bob was fun. There was no doubt that he was a real personality with all sorts of quirks to his character.

Even after a month, he still hated his litter trays. He would scamper away whenever I put one down near him. Instead he would hold on until he saw me going out of the door, and then do his business downstairs in the gardens of the flats.

It wasn't much fun walking down – and up – five flights of stairs to take the cat out whenever he wanted to go to the toilet.

'That's it, Bob,' I told him after three weeks of this. 'You've got to use your litter trays. You can stay inside for twenty-four hours so you've got no choice.'

Bob won that contest hands down. He bottled everything up and waited – and waited and waited – until I had to go out. Then he squeezed past me and bolted down the stairwell to get outside. Game, set and match to Bob. It was a fight I was unlikely to win.

He also had a wild side to his personality. He was calmer than when he'd first arrived, but he still tore around the flat like a complete maniac, playing with anything that he could lay his paws on.

One day he had fun with a bottle top for nearly an hour, flipping it around the floor of the living room with his paws. Another time he found an injured bumblebee struggling around on the coffee table in the living room. Every now and again it would fall off the table on to the carpet. Bob would very gently pick it up with his teeth and put it back on the table, and then watch it while it struggled around again. It was a really comical sight. He didn't want to hurt it. He just wanted to play with it.

He still loved the bins. When I took him downstairs to do his business, he always made a beeline to where the dustbins were kept. I once caught him dragging a chicken drumstick out of a ripped binbag. Old street habits die hard, I figured.

Bob still treated every meal as if it was going to be his last. He guzzled every morsel as if there was no tomorrow.

'Slow down and enjoy your food, Bob,' I laughed.

But it was no use. I guessed he'd spent so long surviving on the streets that he wasn't used to getting a square meal twice a day. I knew how that felt. I'd spent large chunks of my life living the same way. I couldn't really blame him.

Bob and I had so much in common. Maybe that was why the bond had formed so fast – and was growing so deep.

Bob's fur had begun coating every corner of the flat.

Spring was here and he was getting rid of his winter coat. He was rubbing himself on anything he could find in the flat and covering it in a thick film of hair. It was a real pain. But it was a good sign that his coat – and the rest of his body – was returning to good health. He was still a bit scrawny, but I couldn't see his ribs any more. The medication had helped with his bald patches and the antibiotics had healed his old wound. If you didn't know Bob's story, you would never have noticed it.

All in all he looked a lot better than he had done a month or so earlier.

I didn't bathe him. Cats wash themselves, and Bob was a typical cat in that respect. In fact, he was one of the most fastidious cats I'd ever seen. I'd watch him methodically licking his paws and washing himself. It fascinated me, especially because it was linked so strongly to his ancient ancestors.

Bob's distant relatives came from hot climates and didn't sweat, so licking themselves was their way of releasing saliva and cooling themselves down. It was also their version of the invisibility cloak.

Smell is bad for cats. They are stealth hunters and ambush their prey, so they have to be as unobtrusive as possible. Cat saliva contains a natural deodorant, which is why they lick themselves a lot. Zoologists have proved that cats that lick the smell off themselves survive longer. It's also their way of hiding from predators like large snakes, lizards and other carnivorous mammals.

Of course, the most important reason

that Bob and his ancestors had always licked themselves was to stay healthy. Licking cuts down the number of parasites, such as lice, mites and ticks, that can hurt the cat. It also stops infection in any open wounds, as cats' saliva is antiseptic. Perhaps this was why Bob licked himself so regularly. He knew his body had been in a bad way, and he was helping to heal himself.

The other funny habit he'd developed was watching television.

I first noticed that he watched things on screens one day when I was playing around on a computer in the local library. Bob decided to sit on my lap and was staring at the screen with me. I noticed that as I was moving the mouse around, he was trying to swat the cursor with his paw. So I put the TV on as an experiment one day and left the room to go and do something in the bedroom. I came back to find Bob curled up on the sofa, watching.

I'd heard about cats watching TV from Belle, whose cat George (another rescue cat, from Battersea) had loved *Star Trek: The Next Generation*. Before he passed on, whenever he heard the theme tune, he came running into the room and jumped on the sofa. I saw it happen a few times and it was hilarious. No joke.

Pretty soon, Bob became a bit of a telly addict as well. He loved Channel Four racing and the horses in particular. It wasn't something I watched, but I got a real kick from watching him sitting there, fascinated by it.

Chapter 13
Making It Official

I needed to do the responsible thing and get Bob microchipped.

Microchipping cats and dogs used to be complicated but now it's simple. The vet injects a tiny microchip into the cat's neck, which contains a serial number matching the owner's details. That way, if a microchipped cat is found, people can scan the chip and find out where the cat belongs.

Given the life Bob and I led, it was a good idea to get it done. If we ever got separated, we'd be able to find each other. And if something happened to me, the records would show that Bob had once been in a loving home.

When I first looked into microchipping, I knew I couldn't afford it. Most vets charged sixty to eighty pounds to insert a chip, and I didn't have that kind of money. But then one day I got talking to the lady across the street who cared for the stray cats.

'Go to the Blue Cross van in Islington Green on a Thursday,' she said. 'They just charge for the cost of the chip. But make sure you get there early. There's always a big queue.'

As Rose had predicted, Bob and I discovered a long queue when we got to Islington Green early the following Thursday. Luckily it was a bright, clear morning so it wasn't a problem hanging around.

There were people with their cats in posh carriers, and dogs trying to sniff each other and being a nuisance. Bob was the only cat that wasn't in a carrier, so he attracted a lot of attention – as usual.

After about an hour and a half queuing, Bob and I reached the front of the line.

'Good morning,' smiled a young veterinary nurse with short bobbed hair. 'How can we help you today?'

'How much will it cost to get my cat microchipped?' I asked her.

'It's fifteen pounds,' she replied. 'But you don't have to pay it all up front. You can pay it off over a few weeks. Say around two pounds a week, how's that?'

'Cool,' I said, pleasantly surprised. 'I can do that.'

She gave Bob a quick health check. He was looking a lot better, especially now that he had fully shed his winter coat. He was lean and really athletic. Then she led us into the surgery where the vet was waiting.

'Morning,' he said to me before turning to chat to the nurse.

I watched as they got the microchipping stuff together. The size of the syringe and needle to inject the chip took my breath away. It was a big old needle. But it had to be. The chip was the size of a large grain of rice.

Bob didn't like the look of it at all, and I couldn't blame him. He tried to wriggle out of my grip.

'You'll be OK, mate,' I said, stroking his tummy and hind legs.

When the needle went in, Bob let out a loud squeal. It cut through me like a knife. For a moment I thought I was going to start blubbing when he began shaking in pain. But he soon calmed down.

'Well done, mate,' I said.

I gave him a little treat from my rucksack, then carefully scooped him up and headed back to the reception area.

'OK,' said the nurse, 'we need to fill in your details so that they are on the database. Your name, address, age, phone number, all that kind of stuff.'

As I watched the nurse filling in the form, something important struck me.

'So does this mean I am now legally his owner?' I asked.

'Yes,' she smiled. 'Is that OK?'

'Yeah, that's great,' I said, slightly taken aback. 'Really great.'

I gave Bob a stroke on the front of the head. He was obviously still feeling the injection so I didn't go near his neck. He'd have scratched my arm off.

'Did you hear that, Bob?' I said, grinning. 'We're officially a family.'

I'm sure we drew even more looks than usual as we walked through Islington afterwards. I must have been wearing a smile as wide as the Thames.

Having Bob with me had already made a difference to the way I was living my life. He had also made me take a good look at myself. I didn't like what I saw.

I wasn't proud of the fact that I was a recovering heroin addict. So I made it a rule that I didn't take Bob with me on my trips to the drug clinic and the pharmacy for my methadone – the drug that was helping me to kick my heroin habit. It sounds crazy, but I didn't want Bob seeing that side of my past. And, with Bob's help, I really did see it as my past now. I wanted my future to be clean and drug free, and I planned to live a normal life.

A few days after I'd had Bob microchipped, I found a box containing the equipment I had used when I was taking heroin. It was like seeing a ghost. It brought back a lot of bad memories. I saw images of myself that I had never wanted to see again.

'I won't have this box in the house any more,' I decided. I didn't want it around Bob, even though it was hidden away from view.

Bob followed me all the way down to the bin area and watched as I threw the box into a recycling container for hazardous waste.

'There,' I said, turning to Bob who was now fixing me with one of his inquisitive stares. 'Just doing something I should have done a long time ago.'

Chapter 14
The Escape Artist

Life on the streets is never straightforward. You've always got to expect the unexpected. So I wasn't surprised when life around Covent Garden started to get more complicated as that first summer with Bob drew to a close.

Bob was still a real crowd-pleaser, especially with tourists. Wherever they came from, they would stop and talk to him. By now I think I'd heard every language under the sun – from Afrikaans to Welsh – and learned the word for cat in all of them. I knew the Czech name, *kocka*, and the Russian, *koshka*; I knew the Turkish, *kedi*; the Japanese, *neko*; and my favourite, the Chinese, *mao*.

But no matter what weird or wonderful tongue was being spoken, the message was almost always the same. Everyone loved Bob.

But some of the 'locals' were causing the problems.

'This area's for the human statues!' a council official told me as I busked in James Street.

'But there aren't any,' I said, pointing at the empty street.

'You know the rules,' he kept telling me.

124

When you live on the streets, you often bend the rules. So each time I was moved on, I'd go elsewhere for a few hours then quietly slip back into James Street. It was a risk worth taking because I made more money there.

The staff at the tube station had also started complaining about me busking outside their workplace. One really unpleasant inspector, a big, sweaty guy in a blue uniform, came over to me one day.

Bob was a great reader of people. He could spot someone who wasn't quite right from a distance. He spotted this guy the minute he started walking in our direction, and squeezed himself closer to me as he approached.

'You'd better leave or else,' the inspector threatened.

'Or else what?' I said, standing my ground.

'You'll see,' he said, trying to intimidate me. 'I'm warning you.'

The inspector had no power outside the tube station and was just trying to spook me. But I decided that it might be smart to stay away for a while.

At first I moved to the top of Neal Street, out of sight of the tube station staff. The number of people passing there wasn't as great – or always as well-meaning – as the people around Covent Garden. I often got some idiot kicking my bag or trying to scare Bob. Bob would curl up in a defensive ball and narrow his eyes to thin slits whenever I set up there. It was his way of saying: 'I don't like it here.'

So after a few days, rather than

heading towards Covent Garden as usual, Bob and I walked through Soho to Piccadilly Circus instead.

The area to the east of Piccadilly Circus on the road leading to Leicester Square was a good spot for buskers, so I went there. I picked a spot near one of the main entrances to the Piccadilly Circus tube station, outside the Ripley's 'Believe It Or Not' exhibition.

It was a really busy late afternoon and evening with hundreds of tourists on the street, heading to the West End's cinemas and theatres. As usual, people slowed down and sometimes stopped when they saw Bob, and we were soon doing all right. But Bob was nervous, curling himself up even tighter than usual in my guitar case. He preferred being in a place that he recognised.

Everything was fine until around six in the evening, when the crowds really thickened with the beginning of the rush hour. That was when a promotions guy from Ripley's came out on to the street.

He was wearing a big, inflatable outfit that made him look three times his normal size, and was making big arm gestures to encourage people through the doors of the 'Believe It or Not!' exhibition. Bob didn't like the look of him, and I knew exactly where Bob was coming from. The guy looked freaky.

To my relief, Bob settled down and seemed to forget about the man after a while. But then everything suddenly went wrong as he loomed over us.

'Hey there, little guy!' he said, leaning down in his weird inflatable suit to stroke Bob.

Bob sprang up and bolted into the crowds with his new lead trailing behind him. Before I could even react, he'd disappeared towards the entrance to the tube station.

He's gone! I said to myself, my heart pumping. *I've lost him!*

I jumped up straight away and ran after him. I just left the guitar. I was much more worried about Bob.

I immediately found myself in a sea of people. There were weary-looking office workers heading down the tube at the end of a day's work, early evening revellers arriving for a night 'up West' and loads and loads of tourists. I had to bob and weave my way through them to even get to the entrance to the tube station.

It was impossible to see anything through the constant wall of people moving towards me. I finally got to the bottom of the steps inside the concourse, and things began to thin out a little bit. It was still heaving with people, but at least I could now stop and take a look around. I got down and looked around at floor level. One or two people gave me strange looks but I didn't care.

'Bob, Bob, where are you, mate?' I shouted.

It was useless. There was too much noise.

Should I go towards the barriers that led to the escalators and down to the trains, or try the various other exits? Which way would Bob go? My hunch was that he wouldn't go down the tube. We'd never been down there together and the moving escalators would frighten him.

So I moved towards the exits for the other side of Piccadilly Circus.

After a moment or two, I got the faintest flash of ginger on one of the staircases. I then saw a lead trailing after it.

Chapter 15
Together Again

'Bob!' I shouted again, squeezing myself through the crowds. 'Bob!'

I was getting closer to him, but the crowds were so thick that I might as well have been a mile away. There were streams of people coming down the staircase.

'Stop him, step on his lead,' I shouted out, catching another glimpse of ginger in the evening light above me. But no one was paying any attention.

Within moments the lead had disappeared. Bob must have reached the exit, which led to the bottom of Regent Street, and run off from there.

By now a million thoughts were flashing through my head, none of them good. What if Bob had run out into the road at Piccadilly Circus? What if someone had seen him and picked him up? As I barged my way up the stairs and reached street level again I was in a real state. I wanted to burst into tears, I was so convinced that I'd never see him again.

I felt sick. Why hadn't I fixed his lead to my rucksack or on to my belt so that he couldn't run any further than the length of his lead? Why hadn't I spotted his panic when the Ripley's guy had first appeared and moved somewhere else?

Which way next? I guessed that Bob would have headed straight on – down the wider pavements of Regent Street.

Still in a complete panic, I began making my way down the street.

'Have you seen a cat, mate? A ginger cat?'

I asked everyone I passed. I must have looked absolutely crazy.

After about thirty yards, I saw a young woman with a bag from the Apple store at the Oxford Street end of Regent Street. She'd obviously walked all the way down the road.

'Have you seen a cat?' I practically begged.

'Oh yeah,' she said. 'I saw a cat weaving along the street. Ginger. Had a lead hanging behind it. One bloke tried to stamp on the lead and catch it but the cat was too quick for him.'

Bob! My immediate reaction was joy. I could have kissed her. But joy quickly gave way to fear. Who was the bloke who'd tried to catch him? Would that have frightened Bob even more? Was he now somewhere I'd never find him?

With all these new thoughts bouncing around in my head, I carried on down Regent Street, sticking my head into every shop I passed.

'Have you seen a ginger cat?'

Most of the shop assistants looked horrified to see this long-haired figure standing in their doorways. I could see what they were thinking. They thought I was some piece of dirt that had just blown in off the street.

I had no idea how long it was since Bob had run off. Time seemed be happening in slow motion. I was close to giving up.

A couple of hundred yards down Regent Street, there was a side street leading back down to Piccadilly. From there he could have headed in any one of a dozen directions. If he'd gone that far then I knew he was lost.

I stuck my head into a ladies' clothes shop.

'Have you seen a cat?' I asked despairingly.

The two shop assistants' faces lit up.

'A ginger tom?' one of them said.

'Yes! He's got a collar and lead.'

'He's round the back here,' one of them said. 'Come in and shut the door in case he runs out again. We figured someone was looking for him because of the lead.'

They led me towards a row of open wardrobes filled with fancy-looking clothes. Each item cost more money than I'd make in a month. There, in the corner of one of the wardrobes, curled up in a ball, I saw Bob.

Part of me had wondered whether he was trying to get away from me. Maybe he'd had enough. Maybe he didn't want the life I offered him any more. So when I approached him, I was prepared for him to run off. But he didn't.

I'd barely whispered softly, 'Hey Bob, it's me,' before he jumped straight into my arms.

All my fears evaporated as he purred deeply and rubbed himself against me.

'You gave me such a scare there, mate,'

I said, stroking him. 'I thought I'd lost you.'

The two shopkeepers were standing nearby, watching. One of them was dabbing her eyes, close to tears.

'I'm so glad you found him,' she said. 'He looks like such a lovely cat. We were wondering what we'd do with him if no one showed up before closing time.'

She stroked Bob as well. We then chatted for a couple of minutes as she and her colleague got ready to close the till and shut up shop for the evening.

'Bye, Bob,' the pair said as we headed off back into the throng around Piccadilly Circus with Bob perched on my shoulder again.

When I got back to Ripley's, I discovered – to my amazement – that my guitar was still there. Maybe the security guy at the door had kept an eye on it, or a local community support officer. All the police and community support people loved Bob. I was pleased about the guitar, but part of me didn't care. I was just glad that Bob and I were reunited.

I wasted no time in gathering up my stuff and calling it a night. We'd not made much money, but it didn't matter. With most of the cash I had on me, I bought a little belt clip that I attached, first to me, then to Bob's lead. That way we would remain connected all the time.

On the bus, Bob sat on my lap rather than sitting on the seat next to me as usual. I knew exactly what he was thinking because I was thinking it too.

'We're together again. And I hope that never changes."

Chapter 16
Santa Paws

Once or twice after the drama at Piccadilly, Bob decided not to come out with me. When I got the harness out, he ran behind the sofa or hid under the table. He was clearly saying: 'Not today.'

'That's OK, mate,' I told him, and left him to it.

But generally he was still happy to come out every day. I think he felt closer to me now. Our bond had been put to the test – and survived. I got the impression that now he wanted to stay by my side more strongly than ever.

Of course, it wasn't all a bed of roses. A couple of weeks after Bob's scare in Piccadilly, a troupe of street performers came past us in Covent Garden on giant stilts. They were old-fashioned French performance artists and had garish, scary faces.

Bob instantly felt threatened. He squeezed in close to me, flopping his tail over the fretboard of my guitar as I tried to play.

'Cut it out, Bob,' I said. 'Sorry,' I added to the tourists who'd stopped to listen.

'That's really funny!' they laughed, thinking it was part of the act.

As soon as the figures on stilts had gone, Bob relaxed again and moved away from me. He knew that I was his safety net, and I was glad to be.

Our life together had settled into a real routine by Christmas 2007.

Each morning I got up to find Bob waiting patiently by his bowl in the kitchen. He guzzled down his breakfast and then gave himself a good wash, licking his paws and face clean. Most mornings I let him out to do his business. He found his way downstairs and back up again without any trouble. I then packed up my rucksack and grabbed my guitar and we headed into town.

With Christmas only days away, the crowds in Covent Garden were getting bigger. So were the number of treats and gifts Bob was getting.

From the very early days, people had started giving Bob little presents. The first present came from a middle-aged lady who worked in a nearby office.

'I had a ginger tom many years ago,' she sighed when she first stopped to talk to us. 'Bob reminds me of him so much.'

She arrived one evening with a big grin on her face and a smart bag from a fancy pet shop. 'I hope you don't mind, but I bought Bob a little present,' she said, fishing out a little stuffed catnip mouse.

Cats go crazy for catnip. Bob certainly did. The lady stayed for a little while, enjoying the sight of Bob playing with his toy.

As the weather got worse, people began to give Bob more practical presents.

One day a Russian lady sidled up to us, smiling.

'With the weather turning cold, I thought I'd knit Bob something to keep him warm,' she said.

She produced a beautiful, light-blue knitted scarf from her shoulder bag.

'Wow,' I said, genuinely taken aback. 'That's great.'

I immediately wrapped it around Bob's neck. It fitted perfectly and looked fantastic.

The Russian lady was over the moon. She came back a week or two later with a matching blue waistcoat. I was no fashion expert, but even I could tell that Bob looked amazing in it. People were soon queuing to take photographs of him wearing it.

Since then, more than a dozen people had given Bob clothes. One lady even embroidered 'Bob' into a little scarf that she had made for him. Bob was becoming a fashion model. It gave a new meaning to the word 'catwalk'!

It just proved what I'd realised already. I wasn't the only one who loved Bob. He made friends with almost everyone he met. It was a gift I wished I had myself. I'd never found it that easy to bond with people.

No one had fallen more deeply in love with Bob than my friend Belle. She would regularly pop round to the flat, partly to see me and hang out – but also to see Bob. The two of them played together for hours on the sofa. Bob thought Belle was brilliant.

About three weeks before Christmas, Belle came round with a plastic shopping bag in her hand and a big grin on her face.

'What have you got in there?' I asked.

'It's not for you,' she said, teasing me. 'It's for Bob.'

Bob perked up the minute he heard his name.

'Bob, come here, I've got a surprise for you,' Belle said, flopping on to the sofa with the bag.

Bob padded over curiously. Belle pulled out a couple of small animal T-shirts from the bag. One just had a picture of a cute-looking kitten on it. But the other one was red with green trim on it. It had the words 'Santa Paws' in large white letters with a big paw-print underneath it.

'Oh, that's really cool Bob, isn't it?' I laughed. 'It's the perfect thing to wear now it's Christmas. That will really put a smile on people's faces.'

It certainly did that.

I don't know if it was the Christmas spirit or simply seeing Bob in his outfit, but the effect was amazing.

'Ah, look, it's Santa Paws,' people said almost every few minutes.

A lot of people stopped and dropped a bit of silver into my guitar case. Others wanted to give Bob something.

'He's fabulous,' said one very smart lady, stopping to coo over Bob. 'What would he like for Christmas?'

'I have no idea, miss,' I replied.

'Well, put it this way,' she said. 'What does he need?'

'He could do with a spare harness,' I said. 'Or something to keep him warm when the weather gets really cold. Or just get him some toys. Every boy likes toys at Christmas.'

'Jolly good,' she said, getting up and leaving.

I didn't think much more of it, but then, about an hour later, the lady reappeared. She had a big grin on her face and was carrying a smart-looking hand-knitted stocking, with cat designs on the front. I looked inside and could see it was full of goodies: food, toys and stuff.

'You must promise me that you won't open it till Christmas,' she said, stroking Bob. 'You must keep it under your tree until Christmas morning.'

I didn't have the heart to tell her that I didn't have enough money for a Christmas tree or any decorations in the flat. The best I'd been able to rustle up was a ten-inch fibre-optic USB Christmas tree that plugged into the battered old Xbox I'd recently found at a charity shop.

But then I realised that the lady was right. I should have a decent Christmas for once. I had something to celebrate. I had Bob.

I was one of those people who actively dreaded Christmas.

During the past decade, I'd spent most of my Christmases at places like Shelter, where they did a big Christmas lunch for homeless people. It was all very well meaning and I'd had a laugh or two there. But it just reminded me of what I didn't have: a normal life and a normal family. It reminded me that I'd messed up my life.

Once or twice I spent Christmas on my own, trying to forget that my mum was on the other side of the world. On a couple of occasions, I spent it with my father in his house in south London. It wasn't great. He didn't really think much of me and I couldn't blame him. I wasn't exactly a son to be proud about. We didn't do it again.

This year was different though. I invited Belle round on Christmas Eve for a drink. Then for Christmas Day I splashed out on a ready-made turkey breast with all the trimmings. I got Bob some really nice treats, including his favourite chicken meal.

On Christmas Day, we got up reasonably early and went out for a short walk so that Bob could do his business. There were other families from the block heading off to see relatives and friends.

'Happy Christmas!' they said as we passed them.

'Happy Christmas to you too,' we smiled back.

I felt a warmth I'd not experienced in a long while.

Back up at the flat, I gave Bob his stocking.

'Here you go, mate,' I said with a grin.

I emptied the contents one by one. There were treats, toys, balls, and little soft things containing catnip. He absolutely loved it and was soon playing with his new toys like an excitable child on Christmas morning. It was pretty adorable.

I cooked our lunch early in the afternoon, then put a hat on each of us, had a can of beer and watched television for the rest of the afternoon and evening.

It was the best Christmas I'd had in years.

Chapter 17
Mistaken Identity

By the summer of 2008, busking on the streets of London was becoming impossible. The recession was biting and people stopped being generous.

And then the authorities in Covent Garden started coming down hard on street performers like me for playing in the wrong places.

'I'll take away your guitar if you don't

move on!' one guy threatened me.

The staff at Covent Garden tube station started picking on me for busking outside the station as well. It was a constant game of hide and seek, and I was running out of places to hide.

One day, I headed into Covent Garden as usual with Bob. I had a friend called Dylan staying with me at the time.

'Can I come into London and hang out with you guys today?' Dylan said on this particular afternoon. 'It's a lovely, sunny day and I feel like enjoying it.'

Looking back on what happened next, I can't believe how lucky I was that Dylan was there.

I'd barely put the guitar strap over my shoulder when a British Transport Police van pulled up alongside the pavement. Three officers jumped out.

Where our 'tail' began

Time to do your business, Bob

Not much 'fur'ther . . .

Catching the bus by a
whisker and away we go

Bob has the miaow factor

Ready? And . . .

Smile!

Grub's up

Clean paws and claws

Bob's favourite spot

Hmm. What to wear today?

Bob's 'travelcard'

Out on the town

Keeping Bob safe and healthy

Checking his microchip

Look, mate. It's us!

'You're coming with us,' one of the officers said, pointing at me. 'We're arresting you on suspicion of using threatening behaviour.'

They grabbed me. While one of them read me my rights, another one stuck me in handcuffs. My head was spinning. I had no idea what was happening.

'Dylan, will you look after Bob?' I said. 'Take him back to the flat. The keys are in my rucksack.'

Bob looked terrified by what was happening to me. Through the mesh windows at the back of the police van, I watched as the figures of Dylan and Bob standing on the pavement disappeared from view.

I'd had run-ins with the police before, mostly for petty theft. When you are homeless or have a drug habit, you try to find easy ways to make money. My main thing was stealing meat.

The first time I got busted, I had about one hundred and twenty pounds' worth of meat on me that I'd stolen from Marks & Spencer. They fined me eighty pounds for theft. I was lucky to get that because it was my first time.

When you get nicked, it sucks. You try to get out of it and make up lies, but they don't believe you. It's a vicious circle when you are down.

And now here I was, back in trouble. It felt like a real kick in the stomach.

I'd been in a police cell for about half an hour when the door opened suddenly and a white-shirted officer ushered me out. I was taken into a bare room with a few plastic chairs and a single table.

There were a couple of officers sitting opposite me.

'Where were you yesterday evening at around 6.30pm?' one of them asked.

'Busking in Covent Garden,' I said.

'Did you go into the tube station at any time that evening?' the copper asked.

'No, I never go in there,' I said. 'I travel by bus.'

'We have two witnesses who saw you come up the elevator from the tube and try to go through the automatic barrier without a ticket.'

'Well, as I say, that can't have been me,' I said.

'When you were challenged you verbally abused a female member of staff.'

I just sat there shaking my head. This was surreal.

'You were led to the ticket booth and asked to buy a ticket,' he went on. 'You bought a ticket against your will and then spat at the window of the ticket booth.'

'I told you I wasn't in the tube station last night,' I insisted. 'I'm never in there. And I never travel by tube. Me and my cat travel everywhere by bus.'

They just looked at me as if I was telling the biggest lies in the world.

What if this was all a fit-up? What if it went to court and it was my word against three or four London Underground officers?

Worst of all, what would happen to Bob? Who would look after him? Would he head back on to the street? And what would happen to him there? Thinking about it did my head in – he was my baby!

They kept me in for about another two or three hours. I lost all track of time.

'I need to do a DNA test,' said a lady police officer at one point. 'Just sit there and I'll take a swab of saliva from your mouth.'

Eventually, I was let out of the cell and taken back to the desk at the front of the station where I signed for my stuff.

'You have to come back in two days' time,' said the police officer behind the desk. 'Then you'll find out if we are going to charge you.'

Back at the flat, Dylan was watching television with Bob curled up in his usual spot under the radiator. The minute I walked through the door, Bob jumped up and padded over to me, tilting his head to one side and looking up at me.

'Hello, mate, you all right?' I said, dropping to my knees and stroking him.

He immediately clambered up on to my knee and started rubbing against my face.

I sat up for a couple of hours with Dylan, trying to make sense of what had happened to me.

'There's no way they can fix the DNA to match yours, mate,' Dylan reassured me.

I wish I could have been so certain.

I slept fitfully that night, and the night after that. I was due to report at the Transport Police station at midday, but set off early to make sure I was on time.

I didn't want to give them any excuses. I left Bob at home – just in case I was going to be kept there for hours again.

'Don't worry, mate, I'll be back before you know it,' I reassured Bob as I left. If only I'd been as confident as I sounded.

At the police station, it was hard to concentrate on anything. I was eventually called into a room where a couple of officers were waiting for me.

'You'll be pleased to know that we're not going to charge you,' said one of the officers.

'My DNA didn't match the saliva on the ticket collector's booth, did it?' I said.

He just looked at me with a tight-lipped smile.

If that was the good news, the bad news wasn't long in following.

'We are however charging you with illegal busking,' said the other officer. 'Report to court in a week's time.'

I left the station, feeling relieved. Illegal busking wasn't as bad threatening behaviour. I might get away with a small fine and a rap across the knuckles, nothing more. Threatening behaviour might have led to imprisonment.

Part of me wanted to fight back at the injustice of what had happened to me. But the main thought in my mind as I headed home that afternoon was relief and a sense that I'd turned some sort of corner. I wasn't sure yet what it was.

I went to the local Citizens Advice centre and got a bit of legal advice for my court hearing. It was pretty straightforward. I needed to admit that I was guilty of busking: plain and simple. I just had to hope that the magistrate didn't hate street musicians.

When the day came, I put on a clean shirt and had a shave and went to the court.

'James Bowen. The court calls Mr James Bowen,' a plummy-sounding voice announced. I took a deep breath and headed in.

The magistrates looked at me like I was scum. But there wasn't too much they could do to me, especially as it was my first offence for busking.

'But if you reoffend, you will face a fine or worse,' they warned me.

Belle and Bob were waiting for me outside the court-house after the hearing was over. Bob immediately jumped off Belle's lap and walked over to me. It was clear he was pleased to see me.

'How did it go?' Belle asked.

'If I get caught again I'm for the high jump,' I said.

'So what are you going to do?'

I looked at her, then looked down at Bob.

'I don't know, Belle,' I said. 'But the one thing I know I'm not going to do is carry on busking.'

Chapter 18
Number 683

My head was spinning for the next few days. Part of me was still angry at the unfairness of what had happened. But at the same time, I realised that it was a blessing in disguise. I couldn't carry on busking all my life.

So how was I now going to earn money? I didn't have any qualifications. I had some experience with computers, but I hadn't exactly been working for Google and Microsoft for the past ten years. All in all, I was a non-starter when it came to getting a normal job. Whatever normal is.

I needed to make money to look after myself and Bob. So a couple of days after the court hearing, I set off with Bob for Covent Garden without my guitar for the first time in years. When I got to the piazza, I went to find a girl called Sam, the area's *Big Issue* co-ordinator.

I had tried selling the *Big Issue* magazine before, when I first ended up on the streets. I'd lasted less than a year before I gave it up.

I could still remember how difficult it was. I used to sit on a wet and windy street-corner pitch trying to sell my magazines. It was soul-destroying.

'Get a job!' people would snarl at me.

But selling the *Big Issue* IS a job. You are running your own business. People think the *Big Issue* gives the magazines to the sellers for free, but that's not true. I had to buy copies to sell. 'You have to have money, to make money' is as true for *Big Issue* sellers as it is for anyone else.

I never thought I'd try it again. But now I had Bob to think of.

'Hello, you two,' said Sam, the co-ordinator, recognising us and giving Bob a friendly pat. 'Not busking today?'

'Bit of trouble with the cops,' I said. 'Can't risk it now I've got Bob to look after. Can I, mate? So, I was wondering if I could sell the *Big Issue* instead.'

Sam smiled. 'Do you meet the criteria?'

Only a person in 'vulnerable housing' like me was eligible to sell the magazine. I nodded.

'The *Big Issue* offices are down in Vauxhall,' Sam said. 'Go and see them. Once you're badged up, come back here and we can get you going.'

'Better get ourselves organised, Bob,' I said as we headed home. 'We're going for a job interview.'

My housing worker gave me a letter saying that I was living in 'vulnerable housing' and that selling the *Big Issue* would be a good way of helping me get my life back together again. Then I made myself look respectable, tied my hair back, put on a decent shirt and set off for Vauxhall.

I also took Bob with me. He was going

to be part of my team, so I wanted to get him registered as well.

The first thing I noticed when I arrived in the reception area of the *Big Issue* offices was a large sign saying 'No Dogs Allowed'. It didn't say anything about cats, however.

I was interviewed by a decent bloke and we chatted for a while. He'd been on the streets himself years ago.

'I know what it's like out there, James, believe me,' he said. 'Go and have your picture taken and get badged up.'

I went to the next office to see the lady who was issuing the badges.

'Can my cat have an ID card as well?' I asked her.

'Sorry,' she said. 'Pets aren't allowed to have their own badges.'

'Well, what about if he is in the picture with me?' I asked.

She pulled a face, but then she relented.

'Go on then,' she said.

'Smile, Bob,' I said, as we sat in front of the camera.

After waiting about a quarter of an hour, the lady reappeared at the desk.

'Here you go, Mr Bowen,' she said, handing me the laminated badge.

I couldn't help breaking into a big grin at the picture. Bob was on the left-hand side. We were a team. *Big Issue* Vendors Number 683.

It was a long journey back to Tottenham. So I whiled away the time reading through the little booklet they gave me. I was determined to take it more seriously than I had last time.

The *Big Issue* exists to offer homeless and vulnerably housed people the opportunity to earn a legitimate income by selling a magazine to the general public. We believe in offering 'a hand up, not a hand out' and in enabling individuals to take control of their lives.

That's exactly what I want, I said to myself, *a hand up.*

Once they have sold these magazines they can purchase further copies, which they buy for £1 and sell for £2, thereby making £1 per copy.

Each individual must manage their sales and finances carefully. These skills, along with the confidence and self-esteem they build through selling the magazine, are crucial in helping

homeless people back into mainstream
society.

To begin with, I had to work at a 'trial
pitch'. If that went well, I'd get a permanent pitch. I'd also get ten free copies of
the magazine to get me started. Then it
was down to me.

'Everything OK down at Vauxhall?'
Sam asked in Covent Garden the next
morning.

'They gave me one of these,' I grinned,
proudly producing my laminated badge
from under my coat.

'I'd better get you started then,' Sam
said, smiling at the photo of me and
Bob.

She counted out my ten free copies of the magazine.

'There you go,' she said. 'You know you'll have to buy them after this?'

'Yep, I understand,' I said.

I couldn't believe what Sam said next.

'We'll give you the trial pitch just here,' she said, pointing at Covent Garden tube station.

I couldn't stop myself from bursting out laughing.

Sam looked confused. 'Is that a problem? I can find somewhere else.'

'No, it'll be great,' I said. 'A real walk down memory lane.'

I set up immediately. It was mid-morning, and there were lots of people milling around. It was bright and sunny too, which always puts people in a better and more generous mood.

Selling the *Big Issue* was totally different to busking. I was officially licensed to be there. So I stood as close to the tube station as possible without actually being inside, and got on with trying to shift my ten copies of the *Big Issue*.

The tube staff can't give me hassle for this, I thought. *Even if they want to.*

I knew they'd given me this pitch because it was a nightmare. Everyone is in a hurry in a tube station. They have got places to go, people to see. A normal *Big Issue* seller would have done well to stop one in every thousand people that raced past him or her. I'd seen it happen.

But I wasn't a normal *Big Issue* seller. I had a secret weapon, one that had already cast his spell on Covent Garden. And he was soon weaving his magic.

I'd put Bob down on the pavement next to me where he was sitting content-edly watching the world go by. A lot of people didn't notice him as they flew past, but a lot more people did.

Within moments, a couple of young American tourists pulled up to a halt and started pointing at Bob.

'Aaaah,' one of them said, reaching for her camera.

'Do you mind if we take a picture of your cat?' the other one asked.

'Sure, why not?' I said, pleased that they'd had the decency to ask. 'Would you like to buy a copy of the *Big Issue* while you're at it? It will help Bob and me get some dinner tonight.'

'Oh sure,' the second girl said, looking almost ashamed that she'd not thought of it.

'It's no problem if you don't have the money,' I said. 'It's not compulsory.'

But before I could say anything else she'd given me a five-pound note.

'Keep the change and buy your cat something nice to eat,' she smiled.

I sold six copies within the first hour.

Most people gave me the correct money, but one elderly gent in a smart suit gave me a fiver. I knew then that I had made the right move. There would be ups and downs, but I already felt like I'd taken a big step in a new direction.

The icing on the cake came after I'd been there for about two and a half hours. Bob and I were spotted by the large, sweaty Covent Garden ticket attendant who always gave me hassle. He immediately marched in our direction, looking as red as a beetroot.

'What are you doing here?' he shouted. 'I thought you'd been locked up. You know you're not supposed to be here.'

Very slowly and deliberately, I flashed him my *Big Issue* badge.

'I'm just doing my job, mate,' I said, savouring the look on his face. 'I suggest you get on with yours.'

Chapter 19
Pitch Perfect

Becoming a *Big Issue* seller had an immediate impact on life for me and Bob. It gave us more structure for a start.

For those first two weeks, Bob and I worked at Covent Garden from Monday to Saturday. We stayed for as long as it took us to sell a batch of papers. Then the new edition of the magazine would come out each Monday morning.

Being with Bob had already taught me a lot about responsibility. But working for the *Big Issue* took it to another level. From that very first fortnight, I had to run my pitch as a business. I surprised myself with the way I coped with the new demands.

There is no 'sale or return' with the *Big Issue*. That means that if you buy too many, you can lose out quite badly. No one wants to be stuck with fifty papers on Saturday night, with the new magazine coming out on Monday. But if you have too few, you risk selling out too quickly and missing out on willing buyers.

It took a while to get the balance right.

Bob and I were actually making less money than when we were busking. But it was a price worth paying. I was working legitimately on the streets. If I got stopped by a policeman, I could produce my badge and be left in peace. After my experience with the Transport Police, that meant a lot.

The next couple of months working at the tube station flew by.

One day during the early part of the autumn of 2008 we were approached by a very flamboyant-looking guy. I was sure he was an American rock star; he certainly looked like one.

'That's one cool cat,' he said, in a sort of transatlantic drawl.

He spent a minute on his knees just stroking Bob. 'You guys been together long?' he asked.

'It's about a year and a half now,' I told him.

'You look like real soul brothers,' he smiled. 'Like you belong together. Gotta go, see you guys around.'

He reached into a pocket in his jacket and produced a wad of cash. Then he dropped a tenner into my hand.

'Keep the change,' he said. 'You guys have a good day.'

'We will,' I promised him. And we did.

Life on the streets wasn't all sweetness and light. It wasn't a community built on caring for each other, it was a world in which everyone looked after number one. But, to begin with, at least, most of the other *Big Issue* sellers reacted warmly to the sight of the new guy with a cat on his shoulders.

There had always been vendors around with dogs. But, as far as I was aware, there had never been a *Big Issue* seller with a cat in Covent Garden – or anywhere else in London – before.

Some of the vendors were rather sweet about it.

'Where did you guys meet?' they asked me. 'Where did he come from?'

The answer, of course, was that I still didn't know. Bob was a blank slate, a mystery cat, which seemed to endear everyone to him even more.

With Bob at my side I discovered that I could sell as many as thirty or even fifty papers on a good day. At £2 a paper, it could add up quite well, especially with the tips that some people gave me – or, more usually, Bob.

One early autumn evening, Bob was sitting on my rucksack, soaking up the last of the day's sun, when a very well-heeled couple walked past the tube station on their way to the theatre or maybe even the opera. The man was wearing a tuxedo and a bow tie and the lady had a black silk dress on.

'You two look very smart,' I said, as they stopped and started drooling over Bob.

'He's gorgeous,' the lady said. 'Have you been together for a long time?'

'Quite a while,' I said. 'We kind of found each other on the streets.'

'Here you go,' the guy said, suddenly pulling out his wallet and removing a twenty-pound note. 'Keep the change,' he said, smiling at his companion.

The look she gave him spoke volumes. I had a feeling they were on a first date. As they walked off I noticed her leaning into him and wrapping her arm into his.

It was the first time I'd ever been given a twenty-pound drop.

Far from being a 'nightmare' pitch, Covent Garden tube station was actually ideal for me and Bob. But some of the other vendors spotted how well we were doing and became jealous. In our second week, I noticed a subtle but definite change in their attitude towards us.

'Time to move you guys to your permanent pitch,' Sam said at the end of our two-week probation period. 'You can set up on the corner of Neal Street and Shorts Gardens. It's not far.'

I was disappointed, but not surprised. But for once I buttoned my lip and accepted it.

Choose your battles, James, I told myself.

Chapter 20
Under the Weather

It was a cold and wet autumn that year. The biting winds and heavy rains were soon stripping the foliage from the trees.

One morning, as Bob and I set off for the bus stop, a light, fine drizzle was falling. Bob wasn't a big fan of the rain. He seemed to be walking in slow motion.

Maybe he's got second thoughts about joining me today, I thought.

A giant bank of steely, grey clouds were hovering over north London like some vast, alien spaceship. There was almost certainly some heavier rain on its way. It was tempting to turn around, but the weekend was coming and we didn't have enough money to get through it.

Beggars can't be choosers, I said to myself.

Bob was still moving at a snail's pace. It had taken us a couple of minutes to get a hundred yards down the road.

'Come on, mate, climb aboard,' I said.

He draped himself on my shoulder and we trudged on towards the bus.

The rain was already getting worse. We sploshed our way along, ducking under any available shelter as we went. But as we settled into our bus journey, I realised there was more to Bob's low spirits than just the weather.

The bus ride was normally one of Bob's favourite parts of the day. No matter how often we did it, he would never tire of pressing himself against the glass. But today he wasn't even bothered about taking the window seat. Instead he curled up on my lap, which was very unusual. He seemed tired. His body language was droopy. His eyes were drowsy and half asleep. He was definitely not his normal, alert self.

Bob took a distinct turn for the worse when we got off at Tottenham Court Road. As we walked down Neal Street, he started behaving oddly on my shoulder. Rather than sitting there impassively as normal, he was twitching and rocking around.

'You all right there, mate?' I said, slowing down.

All of a sudden he began moving in a really agitated way, making weird retching noises as if he was choking or trying to clear his throat. I was convinced he was going to jump or fall off so I placed him down on the street to see what was wrong.

Before I could even kneel down he began to vomit. It was nothing solid, just bile. But it just kept coming. I could see his body convulsing as he retched and fought to expel whatever it was that was making him sick. For a moment or two I wondered whether it was my fault, and he felt queasy because of all the motion today.

But then he was sick again, retching away and producing more bile. This was more than motion sickness.

All sorts of crazy thoughts rushed

through my mind. Had he eaten something that disagreed with him, or was this something more serious? Was he going to drop dead in front of me? An image of Bob dying flashed through my head. I managed to pull myself together before my imagination ran riot.

Come on, James, let's deal with this sensibly, I told myself.

All the retching meant that Bob was getting dehydrated. He could damage one of his organs if I didn't do something. So I scraped him up and held him in my arms as we walked on to Covent Garden and a general store I knew nearby.

I didn't have much cash, but I cobbled together enough to buy a liquidised chicken meal that Bob usually loved and some mineral water. I didn't want to risk giving him contaminated tap water. That might make matters even worse.

I carried Bob to Covent Garden and put him on the pavement near our normal pitch. I got out his bowl and spooned the chicken into it.

'Here we go, mate,' I said, stroking him as I placed the bowl in front of him.

Ordinarily Bob would have pounced and guzzled everything at once, but not today. Alarm bells started ringing. This wasn't the Bob I knew and loved. Something was definitely wrong.

I half-heartedly set myself up to start selling the magazine. We needed some money to get us through the next few days, especially if I was going to have to take Bob to a vet. But my heart wasn't in it. I was far more concerned with watching Bob than trying to capture the attention of passers-by.

I cut the day short after less than two hours. Bob definitely wasn't right. I had to get him home to the warmth – and dryness – of the flat.

I'd been lucky with Bob until now. Ever since I'd taken him under my wing, he had been in perfect health. He'd had fleas early on, but that was to be expected of a street cat. Since then, he'd suffered no health problems at all. So this was alien territory for me. I was terrified that it might be something serious.

As Bob lay on my lap on the bus returning to Tottenham, I felt the emotions welling up. It was all I could do to stop myself from bursting into tears. Bob was the best thing in my life. The thought of losing him was horrendous. I couldn't keep that thought out of my head.

When we got home, Bob headed for the radiator where he curled up and went straight to sleep. He stayed there for hours. He was too out of it to even follow me to bed.

That night I didn't sleep much, worrying about him. I kept getting up to check on him. One time I was convinced he wasn't breathing, and had to put my hand on him to make sure. I was so relieved when I found he was purring gently.

Money was so tight I simply had to go out again the following day. Should I leave Bob in the flat on his own? Or should I wrap him up warm and take him into central London with me so that I could keep an eagle eye on him?

I didn't know what to do.

Chapter 21
On The Mend

In the morning the weather was a lot better and the sun came out. Bob seemed a bit perkier.

'Do you want a little food, mate?' I asked.

When I offered it to him, he nibbled at it more enthusiastically.

I still couldn't decide what to do. So I headed for the local library where I logged on to a computer and started researching Bob's symptoms.

I'd forgotten what a bad idea it is to search through medical websites. They always give you the worst possible scenario.

When I entered the main symptoms – lethargic, vomiting, appetite loss and a few others – loads of possible illnesses popped up. By the time I'd been reading for fifteen minutes, I was a nervous wreck.

I decided to look at the best treatments for vomiting. The sites I looked at suggested plenty of water, rest and supervision. So that was my plan. I'd keep an eye on him around the clock. If he started vomiting again, I'd head for the vets immediately. If not, I'd go to the Blue Cross van on Thursday.

I stayed at home until late in the afternoon to give Bob a good chance to rest. He slept like a log, curled up in his favourite spot. He seemed OK, so I decided to leave him for three or four hours and try and sell some magazines. I didn't have much option.

Back in Covent Garden, people were concerned to see me on my own.

'Where's Bob?' they asked.

'He's ill,' I told them.

'Is he going to be all right?'

'Is it serious?'

'Is he going to see a vet?'

'Is he OK on his own at home?'

I didn't know.

I suddenly thought of a vet nurse I

knew called Rosemary. Her boyfriend, Steve, worked at a comic-book shop near where we sometimes set up.

I popped into the shop.

'Bob's sick,' I told Steve. 'Do you think it would be OK to call Rosemary for advice?'

'Rosemary won't mind you ringing her,' Steve said. 'Especially as it's about Bob. She loves Bob.'

When I spoke to Rosemary she asked me a load of questions.

'What does he eat? Does he ever eat anything else when he's out and about?'

'Well, he rummages around in the bins,' I said.

It was a habit Bob had never shaken off. You can take the cat off the street, but you can't take the street out of the cat.

'Hmmm,' Rosemary said. 'That might explain it.'

She prescribed some medicine to settle his stomach.

'What's your address?' she said. 'I'll get it biked over to you.'

I was taken aback.

'Oh, I can't afford that, Rosemary,' I said.

'No, don't worry, it won't cost you anything. I'll just add it to another delivery in the area,' she said. 'This evening OK?'

'Yes, great,' I said.

I was overwhelmed. Such kindness hadn't exactly been a part of my life in the past few years. It was one of the biggest changes that Bob had brought with him. Thanks to him I'd rediscovered the good side of human nature. I had begun to place my trust in people again.

Rosemary was as good as her word. The bike arrived early that evening and I administered the first doses of the medicine straight away.

Bob didn't like the taste. He screwed his face up when I gave him his first spoonful.

'Tough luck, mate,' I said. 'If you didn't stick your face in rubbish bins, you wouldn't have to take this stuff.'

The medicine worked straight away. That night Bob slept soundly and was a lot friskier the following morning. I had to hold his head in my hand to make sure he swallowed the next dose.

By the Thursday, he was even better. But just as a precaution, I popped along to see the Blue Cross van on Islington Green.

'Let's give Bob a quick check up, shall we?' said the nurse on duty.

She checked his weight and inside his mouth and had a good feel around his body.

'All seems well,' she said. 'I think he's on the road to recovery. Just don't go rummaging in those bins any more, Bob.'

Seeing Bob sick had a deep effect on me. I'd never imagined him getting ill. Discovering that he was mortal really shook me.

It underlined the feeling that had been building inside me for a while now. It was time for me to get clean.

I was fed up with my lifestyle. I was

tired of feeling like I could slip back into heroin addiction at any time.

I went to see my counsellor.

'I want to come off methadone,' I told him. 'I don't want drugs in my life any more.'

We'd talked about it before, but I don't think he'd ever really believed me. Today, he could tell I was serious.

'Won't be easy, James,' he said.

'Yeah, I know that.'

'You'll need to take a drug called Subutex to begin with,' he said. 'Then we'll slowly decrease that until you don't need to take anything at all.'

'OK,' I said.

'The transition can be hard,' he warned me. 'You can have bad withdrawal symptoms.'

'That's my problem,' I said. 'But I

want to do it. I want to do it for myself and for Bob.'

For the first time in years, I could see the tiniest light at the end of a very dark tunnel.

Chapter 22
The Naughty List

I knew something was wrong the moment Bob and I arrived at the Covent Garden co-ordinators' stand one damp, cold Monday morning

Sam almost always said hello to Bob and gave him a stroke, but not today. She took me to one side.

'James,' she said, looking stern. 'I've had a couple of complaints from the other vendors. You've been spotted "floating" around Covent Garden.'

'Floating' means selling the magazine while you are walking around the streets. It was against the rules of being a *Big Issue* seller. You could sell papers at your pitch, and nowhere else. The other vendors reckoned they'd seen me selling papers while I was walking around with Bob.

'It's not true,' I said.

But I could see why they thought it was.

Wherever we went in London, Bob and I were stopped by people wanting to stroke him or take a photograph. The only difference now was that people would sometimes ask to buy a copy of the *Big Issue* as well.

It didn't take a genius to work out who had reported me.

We had been walking down Long Acre, past a *Big Issue* pitch belonging to a guy called Geoff, when an elderly American couple stopped me and Bob.

'Excuse me, sir,' the husband said, 'but could I take a picture of you and your companion? Our daughter loves cats and it would make her day to see this.'

'Sure,' I said, smiling. No one had called me 'sir' for years – if ever!

I'd got so used to posing for tourists that I'd perfected a couple of poses for Bob that worked best for photographs. I would get him on my right shoulder and turn him to face forward with his face right next to mine. I did this again this morning.

'Oh, gee, we can't thank you enough!' said the wife. 'Our daughter will be thrilled to pieces with that. Can we buy a copy of your magazine?'

'Sorry, no,' I said. I pointed at Geoff a few metres away. 'He is the official *Big Issue* vendor in this area so you'll have to buy it from him.'

'Maybe some other time,' said the husband.

They started walking off. But then the wife leaned towards me and squeezed a fiver into my hand.

'Here you go,' she said. 'Give yourself and your lovely cat a treat.'

'Oi!' Geoff shouted as the couple went off. He jumped to his feet, looking furious. 'What are you doing, taking money?

Who do you think you are, telling people to ignore me? This is MY pitch!'

I knew it looked bad.

'It's not what you think,' I tried to explain.

But I was too late.

'Get out of here, you and your stinking cat!' he screamed. 'Thief! Liar!'

Word of what had happened spread among the other *Big Issue* vendors. Soon they began a whispering campaign against me.

It started with snide remarks.

'Floating around again?'

'Whose sales are you and that mangy moggie going to steal today?'

I kept trying to explain the situation, but it was like talking to a brick wall.

I was really upset by it. I'd made such a huge effort to fit into the *Big Issue* family in Covent Garden. I'd explained time and again what was happening with Bob, but it made no difference. It went in one ear and straight back out the other.

'You are suspended until you sort things out with Head Office,' Sam told me patiently. 'You can't float, James. It's against the rules.'

That was it. I was on the 'Naughty List'.

That night Bob and I ate our dinners and went to bed early. While Bob curled up at the foot of the bed, I huddled under the covers trying desperately to work out what to do next.

If I went to Head Office, would I be banned for good? I'd already lost my busking livelihood. I couldn't lose this as well.

I panicked and decided not to go. Instead, I would try another co-ordinator in a different part of London. It was a risk because I was officially suspended. But I figured it was a risk that was worth taking.

I chanced my arm at Oxford Street, where I'd met a couple of people in the past. I flashed my badge and bought a pile of twenty papers. The guy there was wrapped up in other things, so barely noticed me. I didn't hang around long enough to give him the chance. I simply headed for a spot where there was no sign of anyone else selling, and took my chances.

I managed to sell a decent number of magazines that day – and the same the following day. I moved locations all the time, paranoid, terrified that I was going to lose my job.

I felt sorry for Bob in all this. He was nervous and disoriented. He liked routine, not chaos and uncertainty. So did I. But what choice did I have?

'Why is this happening to us?' I said to Bob as we headed back on the bus one evening. 'We didn't do anything wrong. Why can't we get a break?'

Chapter 23
All Change

I was sitting under a battered old umbrella on a street somewhere near Victoria Station late on a Saturday afternoon when Bob finally told me that I had made a mistake.

It had been hammering down with rain for about four hours and no one had slowed down to stop and buy a magazine. I couldn't blame them.

They just wanted to get out of the deluge.

Selling the paper on the move hadn't been going well. Bob and I had been moved on from various street corners around Oxford Street, Paddington, King's Cross, Euston and other stations.

'This is the third time I've asked you to move,' threatened one police officer. 'I'm giving you a semi-official warning. Next time you'll be arrested.'

I tried to steer clear of the main pitches and pick places off the beaten track. But as a result I'd found it really hard to sell the magazine, even with Bob.

At Victoria Station that day, the light was fading and the rain continued to fall.

'Time to try somewhere else, mate,' I told Bob, packing up. 'We have to shift these papers. They'll be out of date on

Monday and then we're in real trouble.
Let's go.'

Until now Bob had been as good as
gold, even on the grimmest day. He'd
put up with the regular splashings he got
from passing cars and people, even
though he hated getting soaked in the
cold. But when I tried to stop and sit
down at the first street corner we came
to, he pulled on his lead like a dog and
refused to stop walking.

'OK, Bob, I get the message, you don't
want to stop there,' I said. 'We'll try
somewhere else.'

He did exactly the same thing at the
next spot. And then again at the next spot
after that. The penny finally dropped.

'You want to go home, don't you,
Bob?' I said.

He tilted his head in my direction,

giving me what for all the world looked like a raised eyebrow. He then stopped. His expression said:

'That's it. No more. I want to be picked up.'

In that instant, I made the decision. Bob had always stuck loyally by my side, despite the fact that business had been bad and his bowl a little less full of food than before. Now I had to be loyal to him, and get us back on track.

I had to go to Head Office and face the music. For Bob's sake as much as mine. I couldn't keep doing this to him.

The following Monday morning I had a good wash and put on a decent shirt and set off for Vauxhall. Bob came with me.

We sat there for about twenty minutes before a youngish guy and an older woman led us into a nondescript office.

'Shut the door,' said the woman.

I held my breath and waited for the worst.

They gave me a real dressing down.

'We've had complaints that you've been floating and begging,' they said.

'It's been very difficult,' I tried to explain. 'Because of Bob, people stop me and offer to give me money or buy the magazine. It happens all the time. It feels rude to refuse to sell them a paper.'

They listened sympathetically and nodded at some of the points I made.

'We can see that Bob attracts attention,' said the young guy. 'A few vendors have confirmed that he's a bit of a crowd puller. But we still have to give you a verbal warning. It won't stop you from selling, but the situation might change if we find you guilty of floating again.'

That was it?

I felt a bit silly. A verbal warning was neither here nor there. I'd panicked completely and jumped to the worst possible conclusion. I thought I was going to lose my job, but it had never been that serious.

I headed back to Covent Garden.

When Sam the co-ordinator saw me and Bob, she smiled at us.

'Wasn't sure whether we'd see you two again,' she said. 'Been into the office to sort it out?'

'I got a verbal warning,' I told her.

'OK,' she said. 'It looks like you are back on probation. You can only work after 4.30pm and on Sundays for a few weeks. Then we can put you back on a normal shift. If someone comes up to you and Bob and offers to buy a magazine, say you haven't got one, or say they are promised for regular customers.'

It was all good advice.

One Sunday afternoon Bob and I had headed to Covent Garden to do a couple of hours' work. We were sitting near the co-ordinators' spot on James Street when Stan lurched over.

Stan was a well-known figure in *Big Issue* circles. He could be the nicest guy one minute and the biggest pain in the neck the next. It was pain-in-the-neck Stan today.

He was a big guy, nearly two metres tall. He leaned down over me and bellowed: 'You aren't supposed to be here, you are banned from the area.'

'Sam said I could work here on Sunday or after 4.30pm,' I said, standing my ground.

'It's true,' said Peter, another guy who worked on the co-ordinators' stand. 'Leave James alone, Stan.'

Stan lurched back for a moment, then moved back in. He was looking at Bob now, and not in a friendly way.

'If it was up to me, I'd strangle your cat right now,' he said.

His words really freaked me out.

If he'd made a move towards Bob, I would have attacked him. I would have defended Bob like a mother defending her child. Bob was my baby. But that would have been the end, from the *Big Issue*'s point of view. I would never have worked for them again.

I made two decisions there and then. I decided that I couldn't work anywhere near Stan when he was in this mood. But I also made the decision to move away from Covent Garden.

It would be a wrench. Bob and I had a loyal customer base there. But we needed to move to a less competitive part of London, somewhere where we weren't so well known.

I used to busk around the Angel tube station in Islington before I went to Covent Garden. It was a good area. So I decided the next day to visit the co-ordinator there.

'You could do outside the tube station if you like,' the co-ordinator said when I asked him about getting a pitch. 'No one fancies it much.'

I had a feeling of déjà vu.

As I'd discovered at Covent Garden, Bob had the magical ability to slow people down at a tube station. People would see him and suddenly they weren't in quite such a rush. It was as if he was providing them with a little bit of light relief, a little bit of warmth and friendliness. I'm sure a lot of people bought a *Big Issue* as a thank you for Bob giving them that little moment. So I was more than happy to take what was supposed to be a 'difficult' pitch, right outside Angel tube.

We started that same week.

Almost immediately we began to get people slowing down to say hello to Bob. We had soon picked up where we had left off in Covent Garden.

One or two people recognised us.

One evening, a well-dressed lady in a business suit stopped and did a sort of double take.

'Don't you two work in Covent Garden?' she said.

'Not any more, madam,' I said with a smile, 'not any more.'

Chapter 24
Angel Hearts

Bob was very happy about the move to Angel.

When we got off the bus at Islington Green, he wouldn't ask to climb on my shoulders like in central London. Instead, most mornings he would take the lead and march ahead of me, down Camden Passage, past all the antique stores, cafés, pubs and restaurants, and along towards the end of Islington High Street and the large paved area around the tube station entrance.

Sometimes we headed to the *Big Issue* co-ordinator on the north side of the Green. Then Bob always made a beeline for the enclosed garden area at the heart of the Green. I'd wait and watch while he rummaged around in the under-growth, sniffing for rodents and birds. He loved sticking his head into every nook and cranny in the area.

When we eventually arrived at his favourite spot, facing the flower stall and the newspaper stand by the entrance to the Angel tube station, he would watch me put my bag down on the pavement with a copy of the *Big Issue* in front of it. Then he would sit down, lick himself clean from the journey and get ready for the day.

I felt the same way about our new stamping ground. Islington was a fresh start, and this time it was going to last.

The Angel was different from Covent Garden and the streets around the West End. There were still a lot of tourists, but it was more professional and 'upmarket'. Each evening, hordes of people in business suits headed in and out of the tube station. Most of them barely noticed a ginger cat sitting outside the station. But lots of others took an instant shine to Bob. They were also really generous. The average purchase and tip at Islington was just that little bit bigger than in Covent Garden.

The Angel locals were also generous. Almost as soon as we began selling the *Big Issue* there, people began giving Bob bits of food.

The first time it happened was on our second or third day. A very smartly dressed lady stopped for a chat.

'Are you going to be here every day?' she asked.

This worried me. Was she going to make some sort of complaint? But I was completely off the mark. The following day she appeared with a small supermarket bag containing some cat milk and a pouch of cat food.

'There you go, Bob,' she said happily, placing them on the pavement in front of Bob.

After that, more and more locals started donating titbits for him.

Our pitch was down the road from a large supermarket. People went in there to do their normal shopping and picked up a little treat for Bob. They then dropped their presents off on their way back home.

Just a few weeks after we began at Angel, about half a dozen different people did this. By the end of the day, I couldn't fit all the tins of cat milk, pouches of food and tins of tuna and other fish into my rucksack. I had to keep it all in a large supermarket bag. When I got back to the flat, it filled up an entire shelf in one of the kitchen cupboards. It kept us going for almost a week.

Unlike Covent Garden, the staff at the Angel tube station were really warm and generous towards Bob from the very beginning. One day, for instance, the sun was blazingly hot and I was sweating like crazy in my jeans and black T-shirt. I put Bob in the shade of the building behind us, but he needed some water. Before I was able to do something, a figure appeared from inside the tube station with a nice clean, steel bowl brimming with clear water. It was Davika, one of the ticket attendants. She'd stopped to talk to Bob lots of times already.

'Here you go, Bob,' she said, stroking him on the back of the neck as she placed the bowl in front of him. 'Don't want you getting dehydrated now, do we?'

Bob wasted no time in lapping it up.

Bob had always endeared himself to people, but he won the Islington crowd over in a matter of weeks. It was amazing.

Of course, it wasn't perfect at the Angel. This was London, after all.

Unlike Covent Garden, things were

concentrated around the tube at the Angel. As a result there were a lot of other people working on the streets, dishing out free magazines and collecting for charities.

One day I got into a heated argument with a young curly-haired student who was a 'chugger' – a charity worker who collected people's details for charity donations. He'd been really irritating people by bouncing around and walking alongside them as they tried to get away. I decided to have a word.

'Hey, mate, you're making life difficult for the rest of us who are working here,' I said. 'Can you just move along the road a few yards and give us some space?'

'I've got every right to be here,' he complained. 'I will do what I want.'

'You're just trying to make pocket

money for your "gap year",' I pointed out. 'I'm trying to make money to pay for my electricity and gas and to keep a roof over my and Bob's heads.'

His face kind of sank when I put it like that.

I was the only licensed vendor in the area outside the tube station. But the chuggers, hawkers and bucket rattlers didn't seem to care.

But still, it was a good move. I was glad Bob and I had made it.

Now I just had one more hurdle to face. It was time to bring an end to my drug addiction, once and for all.

Chapter 25
Forty-eight Hours

The young doctor at the DDU – the drug dependency unit – scribbled his signature at the bottom of the prescription.

'Take this and come back in forty-eight hours,' he said. 'It's going to be tough, but it will be a lot tougher if you don't stick to what I've said. OK?'

At last, my counsellors and doctors

had agreed that I could take the final step towards life without drugs. This was my last prescription for methadone, which had helped me kick my dependence on heroin. In forty-eight hours, I would be given my first dose of a milder drug called Subutex, to ease me out of drug dependency completely.

'You will have bad physical and mental withdrawal symptoms,' said the counsellor. 'You have to wait for those symptoms to become quite severe before you can come back to the clinic for your first dose of Subutex. If you don't do this, you risk a much worse withdrawal.'

I was confident that I could do it. I *had* to do it.

Ten years of my life had already slipped away. When you are reliant on drugs, minutes become hours, hours

become days. You only start worrying
about it when you need your next fix.
You don't even care until then. I didn't
want that any more.

I had Bob to think about.

As usual, I didn't take Bob with me to
the drug clinic. It was a part of my life I
wasn't proud about.

When I got home he was pleased to
see me, especially as I had a bag full of
supermarket goodies to get us through
the next two days. Anyone who is trying
to get rid of an addictive habit knows
what it is like. The first forty-eight hours
are the hardest. The trick is to think of
something else. I was really grateful that
I had Bob to help me do just that.

That lunchtime we sat down in front
of the television, had a snack together –
and waited.

The methadone lasted for around twenty hours, so the first part of the day passed easily. Bob and I played around a lot and went out for a short walk. I played a really old version of the original *Halo 2* game on my knackered old Xbox. At that point it was all plain sailing. It couldn't stay that way for much longer.

The withdrawal symptoms kicked in twenty-four hours after my final dose of methadone. Eight hours later, I was sweating and feeling twitchy. It was the middle of the night and I should have been asleep. I did nod off but I felt like I was conscious all the time.

I had dreams of trying to take heroin, but something always going wrong at the last minute. My body knew that it wasn't being given the drug that it wanted. Deep in my brain, a huge battle of wills was going on.

Moving from heroin to methadone years ago hadn't been so bad. This was a different experience altogether.

By the following morning, I was getting really bad headaches, almost migraines. I found it hard to cope with any light or noise. I'd try and sit in the dark, but then I'd start hallucinating and want to snap myself out of it. It was a vicious circle.

Bob was my salvation.

It was like he could read my mind. He knew that I needed him, so he was always there. He knew what I was feeling. Sometimes I'd be nodding off and he would come up to me and place his face close to me, as if to say:

'You all right, mate? I'm here if you need me.'

At other times he would just sit with me, purring away, rubbing his tail on me and licking my face every now and again. He anchored me to reality.

He was a godsend in other ways too. For a start, he gave me something to do. I still had to feed him, which I did regularly. Going into the kitchen, opening up a sachet of food and mixing it in the bowl was just the sort of thing I needed to get my mind off what I was going through. I didn't feel up to going downstairs to help him do his business, but when I let him out he dashed off and was back upstairs again in what seemed like a few minutes. He didn't want to leave my side.

During the morning of the second day, I didn't feel so bad. Bob and I played

for a couple of hours. I did a bit of reading. It was hard, but it kept my mind
occupied. I read a really good non-fiction
book about a Marine saving dogs in
Afghanistan. It was good to think about
what was going on in someone else's life.

But by the afternoon and early evening
of the second day, the withdrawal symptoms were becoming unbearable. The
worst thing was the physical stuff. I
started doing this thing where my legs
would suddenly start kicking. It's not
called kicking the habit for nothing. It
freaked Bob out, and he gave me a
couple of odd, sideways looks. But he
didn't desert me.

That night was the worst of all. I
couldn't watch television because the
light and noise hurt my head. My mind
was racing, filling up with all kinds of

crazy stuff. One minute I was so hot I felt like I was inside a furnace. The next I'd feel ice cold. The sweat that had built up all over me would suddenly start to freeze and then I'd be shivering. So then I'd have to cover up and would start burning up again. And all the time, my legs were kicking. It was a horrible cycle.

I understood why so many people find it so hard to kick their drug habits. I saw – and smelled – the alleys and under-passes where I'd slept rough, the hostels where I'd feared for my life, the terrible things I'd done. I saw just how seriously addiction screws up your life.

I won't deny that I had moments of weakness. But I fended off thoughts of giving up. I had to stay strong, I had to take it: the diarrhoea, the cramps, the vomiting, the headaches, the hot and cold temperatures – all of it.

That second night seemed to last forever. The clock seemed to be moving backwards. The darkness seemed to be getting deeper and blacker rather than brightening up for morning. It was horrible.

But I had my secret weapon. Bob.

At one stage I was lying as still and quiet as possible, just trying to shut out the world. All of a sudden, I felt Bob clawing at my leg, digging into my skin quite painfully.

'Bob, what are you doing?' I shouted, making him jump.

Immediately I felt guilty. Bob was just worried that I was too still and quiet, and was checking to make sure I was alive. He was worried about me.

Eventually, a thin, soupy grey light

began to seep through the window. Morning had arrived at last. I hauled myself out of bed. It was almost eight o'clock. The clinic would be open by nine. I couldn't wait any longer.

Getting the bus from Tottenham to Camden at that time of the day was always bad. Today it seemed much worse. People were looking at me as if I was some kind of nutcase. I probably looked unbelievably bad. I didn't care. I just wanted to get to the DDU.

I arrived just after nine and found the waiting room half full already. One or two people looked as rough as I felt. Perhaps they'd been through the same forty-eight hours as me.

'Hi, James, how are you feeling?' the counsellor said as he came into the treatment room.

'Not great,' I said.

'Well, you've done well to get through the last two days. That's a huge step you've taken,' he smiled.

He checked me over and I gave a urine sample. He then gave me a tablet of Subutex and scribbled out a new prescription.

'That should make you feel a lot better,' he said. 'Now let's start easing you off this – and out of this place completely.'

By the time I got back to Tottenham, I felt completely transformed. The world seemed more vivid. I could see, hear and smell more clearly. Colours were brighter. Sounds were crisper. It may sound strange, but I felt more alive again.

I stopped on the way and bought Bob a couple of new-flavoured Sheba pouches that had come on to the market. I also bought him a little toy, a squeezy mouse.

Back at the flat I made a huge fuss of him.

'We did it mate,' I said. 'We did it.'

The sense of achievement was incredible. Over the next few days, the transformation in my health and life was huge. It was as if someone had drawn back the curtains and shed some sunlight into my life.

Of course, in a way, someone had. It was Bob.

Chapter 26
Homeward Bound

What Bob and I had just been through together tightened our bond even more. In the days that followed, Bob stuck to me like a limpet, watching over me in case I had a relapse.

But there was no danger of that.

I celebrated my breakthrough by doing up the flat. Bob and I put in a few extra hours each day outside the tube station, and then bought some paint, a few cushions and a couple of prints to put on the walls.

In a good second-hand furniture shop in Tottenham, I bought a nice sofa. The old one was knackered, partly because of Bob's habit of scratching at its legs and base. Bob was banned from scratching the new one.

I was already looking forward to a nice Christmas for me and Bob. But as it turned out, that was a little premature.

One morning in early November 2008, I got a letter. It was an airmail envelope and had a postmark – Tasmania, Australia.

It was from my mother.

Dear James,
How are you? I haven't heard from you in a long time. I've moved to a new house in

Tasmania, where I'm very happy. It's a little farm way out in the middle of nowhere, by a river. If I pay your air fares to Australia and back, will you come and see me? You could come during the Christmas holidays. Maybe you could go to Melbourne as well, to see your godparents. You were always very close. Let me know.

Lots of love,

Mum

In the past, I would have thrown the letter straight into the dustbin. I was too proud and stubborn to accept help from my family. But now my head was in a different place. I decided to give it some thought.

It was a difficult decision. There were lots of pros and cons.

The biggest pro was that I'd see Mum

again. We'd had ups and downs in the past, but she was my mother and I missed her.

I'd never been honest with Mum about what had happened to me. The last time she had come to London, we met for a few hours and I told her a pack of lies.

'I've got a band in London,' I told her. 'I'm not coming back to Australia just yet, because we're trying to make it big.'

I didn't have the courage or the strength to tell her that I was sleeping rough, hooked on heroin and wasting my life away.

I used to go for months on end without contacting her. Heroin does that to you. You don't think about anyone but yourself. This trip to Australia was a chance to make it up to her and to put the record straight.

I'd also get a decent holiday in the sun – something I hadn't had for years. But what about Bob? Who would look after him? Would he still be waiting for me when I got back? Did I want to be separated from my soul mate for weeks on end?

'Mum's invited me for a holiday in Australia,' I told my friend Belle. 'I want to go, but I don't know what to do about Bob.'

'I'll look after him at my flat,' Belle said at once.

I knew Belle was trustworthy and would take care of Bob. But I still wondered what the effect would be on him if I went away.

I was also worried about money. Even

though Mum had offered to pay for my fare, I needed at least £500 in cash before they would let me into the country.

After weighing it up for a few days, I decided to go.

I got a new passport with the help of a social worker, and sorted out the flights. The cheapest deal was to fly to Beijing and then down to Melbourne. I sent Mum an email with all the details, including my new passport number. A few days later I got a confirmation email about my tickets. I was on my way.

All I had to do now was raise £500. Easy – or so I hoped.

For the next few weeks, I worked every hour of the day in all weather. Bob came with me most days, although I left him at home when it was raining heavily. I knew he didn't like it, and I didn't want to risk him getting ill before I went away. There was no way I'd be able to go to Australia knowing he was ill again.

I was soon saving up a bit of cash, and at last I had enough to make the trip.

'Bye, Bob,' I said at Belle's flat. I had a heavy heart. 'Be good. Don't forget me.'

Bob didn't look too concerned. But then he had no idea I was going to be away for nearly six weeks. He'd be safe with Belle, but it still didn't stop me fretting. I really had become a paranoid parent, just like a lion with its cubs.

If I'd imagined the trip to Australia was going to be relaxing, I was sorely mistaken. It took me thirty-six hours, and was an absolute nightmare. By the time I got to Tasmania, I was utterly exhausted.

But seeing my mother was wonderful. She was waiting at the airport and gave me a couple of really long hugs. She was crying. She was pleased to see me alive, I think.

The house was a big, airy bungalow with a huge garden space at the back. It was surrounded by farmland with a river running by the bottom of her land. It was a very peaceful, picturesque place. Over the next month I just hung out there, relaxing and recovering.

Within a couple of weeks I felt like a different person. The anxieties of London were – literally – tens of thousands of miles away. My Mum made sure I ate well, and looked after me. At last, we started repairing our relationship.

One night as we sat on the back porch, watching the sun go down, everything came out. It wasn't a big confession, there was no Hollywood drama. I just talked . . . and talked.

As I explained what I'd been through over the last ten years, Mum looked horrified.

'I guessed you weren't doing so great when I saw you, but I never guessed it was that bad,' she said, close to tears. 'Why didn't you tell me you'd lost your passport? Why didn't you call me and ask for help? Why didn't you contact your father? It's all my fault, isn't it? I let you down.'

'No . . . I let myself down,' I told her. 'You didn't decide I should sleep in cardboard boxes and take drugs every night. I did.'

The ice was broken. We talked about the past and my childhood in Australia and England. We laughed a lot too; it wasn't all dark conversation. We admitted how similar we were and chuckled at some of the arguments we used to have when I was a teenager.

'I'm a strong personality and so are you,' Mum said. 'That's where you get it from.'

She asked me all sorts of questions about my rehab process, and about getting off the drugs.

'It's still a case of taking one step at a time,' I told her. 'But with luck, I'll be totally clean within a year or so.'

During those long chats, I often talked about Bob. I'd brought a photo of him with me, which I showed everyone and anyone who took an interest.

'He looks a smart cookie,' my mother smiled when she saw it.

'Oh, he is,' I said, beaming with pride. 'I don't know where I'd be now if it wasn't for Bob.'

There was a part of me that hankered to move back to Australia. But I kept thinking about Bob. He'd be as lost without me as I'd be without him. I didn't take the idea seriously for very long. By the time I'd started my sixth week away, I was mentally already on the plane back to England.

Mum came to the airport with me and waved me off on my way to Melbourne, where I spent some time with my godparents. They were as shocked as my mother to hear my story.

'We'll help you financially,' they promised. 'We'll find you work in Australia.'

'Thanks for the offer,' I said, smiling. 'But I have responsibilities back in London. It's time for me to go back.'

I was so rested and revived by my time in Australia that I slept for most of the trip home.

I was dying to see Bob again, although a part of me was worried that he might have changed or even forgotten me. I needn't have had any concerns.

The minute I walked into Belle's flat, his tail popped up and he bounced off her sofa and ran up to me.

'Here you go, mate,' I grinned, stroking him over and over. I'd brought him back a few little presents, a couple of stuffed kangaroo toys. He was soon clawing away at one of them.

As we headed home that evening, he scampered up my arm and on to my shoulders as usual. In an instant, the emotional and physical journey I'd made to the other side of the world was forgotten. It was me and Bob against the world once more. It was as if I'd never been away.

Chapter 27

The Stationmaster

Back in London, I felt stronger and more sure of myself than I'd felt in years. Being reunited with Bob had lifted my spirits even more. Without him, a little part of me had been missing down in Tasmania. Now I felt whole again.

We were soon back into the old routine. Even now, after almost two years together, he surprised me all the time.

I'd talked endlessly about Bob while I was away, telling everyone how smart he was. There had been times when people thought I was crazy. 'A cat can't be that smart,' I'm sure they were thinking.

A couple of weeks after I got back, however, I realised that I'd been under-selling him.

Doing his business had always been a bit of a chore for Bob. He'd never taken to the litter trays that I'd bought him. I still had a few packs of them in the cupboard gathering dust. They'd been there since day one.

It was a real pain having to go all the way down five flights of stairs and out into the grounds every single time he needed to go to the loo. I'd noticed in the past few months, before I'd gone to Australia and again now that I was back, that he wasn't going to the toilet downstairs so often any more.

For a while I wondered whether he had a medical problem. I took him to the Blue Cross van on Islington Green to check him over.

'He's fine,' the vets assured me. 'It might just be a change in his metabolism now that he's getting older.'

The explanation was much funnier than that.

Soon after I'd got back from Australia, I woke up really early because my body clock was still all over the place. I hauled myself out of bed and stepped, bleary-eyed towards the toilet. The door was half open and I could hear a light, tinkling sort of noise.

Weird, I thought.

Had someone sneaked into the flat to use the toilet?

When I gently nudged open the door I was greeted by a sight that left me totally speechless. Bob was squatting on the toilet seat.

He had obviously decided that going to the toilet downstairs was too much hassle. So, having seen me go to the toilet a few times in the past two years, he'd worked out what he needed to do and simply copied me.

When he saw me staring at him, Bob just fired me one of his withering looks.

'What are you looking at?' he seemed to say. 'I'm only going to the loo. What could be more normal than that?'

He was right of course. Why was I

surprised at anything Bob did? He was capable of anything. Surely I knew that already?

A lot of the locals at the Angel had noticed our absence.

'Ah, you're back!' they said during our first week back at our pitch. 'We thought you'd won the lottery!'

One lady dropped off a card with 'We Missed You' written on it. It felt great to be 'home'.

Of course, there were also one or two who weren't so pleased to see us.

One evening I got into a heated argument with a Chinese lady. I'd noticed her before, looking disapprovingly at me and Bob. This time she approached me, waving her finger at me as she did so.

'This not right, this not right,' she said angrily.

'Sorry, what's not right?' I said, genuinely baffled.

'This not normal for cat to be like this,' she went on. 'Him too quiet, you drug him. You drug cat.'

Other people had thought this back in Covent Garden too.

'I'm on to you,' said a snotty professor-type guy who'd stopped by one day. 'I know what you're doing. I know what you're giving him to stay so docile and obedient.'

'And what would that be then, sir?' I said.

'I'm not telling you,' he said, a bit taken aback that I was challenging him. 'You'll just change to something else.'

'No, come on, you've made an accusation, now back it up,' I said, stepping up my defence.

He disappeared into thin air fairly quickly.

The Chinese woman was basically making the same accusation. So I gave her the same defence.

'What do you think I am giving him that makes him like that?' I said.

'I don't know,' she said. 'But you giving him something.'

'Well, if I was drugging him, why would he hang around with me every day?' I said. 'Why wouldn't he try and make a run for it when he got the chance? I can't drug him in front of everyone.'

'Psssh,' she said, waving her arms at

me and turning on her heels. 'It not right, it not right,' she said once more as she melted into the crowd.

There were always people who were suspicious that I was mistreating Bob. A couple of weeks after the row with the Chinese lady, I had another confrontation, but a very different one this time.

Since the early days in Covent Garden, I'd regularly been offered money for Bob. Every now and again someone would come up to me and ask, 'How much for your cat?' I'd usually tell them where to go.

Up here at the Angel I heard it again, from one lady in particular. She came to see me several times, each time chatting away before getting to the point of her visit.

'Look, James,' she said. 'Bob shouldn't

be out on the streets. He should be in a nice, warm home, living a better life. How much do you want for him? A hundred pounds? Five hundred?'

At last she came up to me one evening and said: 'I'll give you a thousand pounds for him.'

I'd just looked at her. 'Do you have children?' I asked.

'Erm, yes, as a matter of fact I do,' she spluttered, a bit thrown.

'OK. How much for your youngest child?'

'What are you talking about?'

'How much for your youngest child?'

'I hardly think that's got anything to do—'

I cut her off. 'Actually, I think it does have a lot to do with it. As far as I'm concerned, Bob is my child. You asking me to sell him is *exactly* the same as me asking you how much you want for your youngest child.'

She stormed off. I never saw her again.

The attitude of the tube station staff was the complete polar opposite of this. One day I was talking to one of the ticket inspectors, Leanne.

'He's putting Angel tube station on the map, isn't he?' she laughed, chuckling at the way countless people stopped and took Bob's picture.

'He is,' I agreed. 'You should put him on the staff, like that cat in Japan who is a stationmaster. He even wears a hat.'

'I'm not sure we've got any vacancies,' she giggled.

'Well, you should at least give him an ID card or something,' I joked.

She looked at me with a thoughtful look on her face and went away. I thought nothing more about it.

A couple of weeks later Bob and I were sitting outside the station one evening when Leanne appeared again. She had a big grin on her face. I was immediately suspicious.

'What's up?' I said.

'Nothing, I just wanted to give Bob this,' she smiled. She then produced a laminated travel card with Bob's photograph on it.

'That's fantastic,' I said.

'I got the picture off the Internet,' she said, to my slight amazement. What was Bob doing on the Internet?

'It means that he can travel as a passenger for free on the underground,' she went on, laughing.

'I thought that cats went free anyway?' I smiled.

'Well, it actually means we are all very fond of him. We think of him as part of the family.'

It took a lot of willpower to stop myself from bursting into tears.

Chapter 28
Big Trouble

Living on the streets of London gives you really well-developed radar when it comes to sussing out people you should avoid at all costs. It was around 6.30 or 7pm, during the busiest part of the day for me, when a guy fitting that description loomed into view at the Angel tube station.

He was a really rough-looking

character. His skin was all red and blotchy and his clothes were smeared in dirt. But what really stuck out about him was his dog, a giant black and brown Rottweiler. From the moment I first saw it, I could tell that it was aggressive.

Almost immediately the Rottweiler spotted Bob. It strained at the lead, dying to come and have a go at him. The guy seemed to have the big dog under control, but how long was that going to last?

I wanted to get myself and Bob as far away from them as possible.

I began gathering up my *Big Issue*s and placing my other bits and pieces in my rucksack. All of a sudden I heard this really loud, piercing bark.

I turned round to see a flash of black and brown heading towards me and Bob. The Rottweiler was on the loose.

I had to protect Bob! So I jumped in front of the dog. Before I knew it, the Rottweiler had run into me, bowling me over. We ended up on the floor, wrestling. I was trying to get a good grip on its head so that it couldn't bite me, but the dog was simply too strong.

'Come here, you!'

The owner yanked as hard as he could on the Rottweiler's lead. He then walloped the dog across the head with something blunt. The sound was sickening. In different circumstances I'd have been worried for the dog's welfare, but my main priority was Bob. He must have been terrified.

I turned to check on him. The spot where he'd been sitting was empty.

I spun around to see if someone had perhaps picked him up to protect him, but there was no sign of him. Bob had disappeared.

Suddenly, I realised what I'd done. I had unclipped Bob's lead from my belt in order to reach my magazines and pack them away more quickly. It had only been for a second or two, but that had been long enough. The Rottweiler must have seen me do it, and realised that Bob was off his leash. That's why he'd broken free and charged at us at that precise moment.

I was immediately thrown into a blind panic.

'Has anyone seen Bob?' I gasped.

'I just saw him running off towards Camden Passage,' said a regular customer of mine, a middle-aged lady who often gave Bob treats. 'I tried to grab his lead but he was too quick.'

'Thanks,' I said.

I grabbed my rucksack and ran, my chest pounding.

My mind immediately flashed back to the time Bob had run off in Piccadilly Circus. For some reason, this felt like a more serious situation. Back then, he had basically been spooked by a man in a funny outfit. This time he'd been in real physical danger. If I hadn't intervened, the Rottweiler would almost certainly have attacked him. I guessed he was as frightened and distressed as me.

I ran straight towards Camden Passage, dodging the early evening crowds milling around the pubs, bars and restaurants.

'Bob, Bob,' I kept calling, drawing looks from passers-by. 'Anyone seen a ginger tom running this way with his lead trailing after him?' I asked a group of people standing outside a pub.

They all just shrugged their shoulders.

I had hoped that Bob would find refuge in a shop, like in Piccadilly Circus. But most of them were shuttered up for the evening. Only the bars, restaurants and cafés were open.

If Bob was still heading this way, he was going to end up on the main road. He'd walked part of that route before, but never at night or on his own.

I was beginning to despair when I met a woman near Islington Green. She pointed down the road.

'I saw a cat running down that way,' she said. 'It was going like a rocket, veering towards the main road. It looked like it was thinking about crossing.'

Bob was fond of Islington Green, and often stopped to do his business there. It was also where the Blue Cross vans parked. It was worth a look.

I quickly crossed the road and ran into the small, enclosed grassy area. I knelt down and looked among the bushes. Even though the light had gone and I was barely able to see my hand in front of me, I hoped against hope that I might see a pair of bright eyes staring back at me. There was nothing.

I walked down to the other corner of the enclosed Green and shouted a couple more times.

'Bob! Bob, mate! It's me!'

But all I could hear was the insistent droning of the traffic.

I found myself facing the big Waterstone's bookshop. Bob and I often popped in there and the staff always made a fuss of him. I was clutching at straws now, but maybe he had headed there for refuge.

It was quiet inside the store and some of the staff were getting ready to shut up for the evening. There were just a few people browsing the shelves.

By now I was sweating and breathing heavily.

'Are you all right?' asked a lady I recognised behind the till.

'I've lost Bob,' I panted. 'A dog attacked us and Bob ran off. He didn't come in here, did he?'

'Oh, no,' she said, looking genuinely concerned. 'I've been here and I've not seen him. I'm really sorry. If we do see him we'll make sure to keep him.'

'Thanks,' I said.

It was only then, as I wandered back out of Waterstone's and into the now dark evening, that it hit me.

I've lost him.

Chapter 29
The Longest Night

For the next few minutes I was in a daze. I carried on walking down the main road. When I saw a bus bound for Tottenham, another thought formed in my frazzled mind. He couldn't have? Could he?

'Have you seen a cat getting on a bus?' I asked an inspector at one of the stops.

I knew Bob, he was smart enough to do it. But the guy just looked at me like I'd asked him whether he'd seen aliens getting on the number 73. He shook his head and turned away.

Cats have a great sense of direction, and have been known to make long journeys. But there was no way Bob could get all the way back to Tottenham on foot. It was a good three and a half miles. We'd never walked it, we'd only ever done it on the bus. I quickly decided that was impossible.

The next half hour or so was a rollercoaster of conflicting emotions.

He won't stray far without being found and identified, I convinced myself. *Loads of local people know who he is. And even if they don't know him, they'll see that he's microchipped. I'll get him back.*

But the wilder, more irrational side of me was saying something much bleaker. It was saying: 'He's gone, you won't see him again.'

I wandered up and down the main road for nearly an hour. It was now pitch dark, and I was all at sea. I didn't know what to do. Without thinking, I started walking towards Dalston and my friend Belle's flat.

I was walking past an alleyway when I saw a flash of a tail. It was black and thin, very different to Bob's, but I was in such a state that my mind was playing tricks.

'Bob,' I shouted, diving into the dark space. But there was nothing there. After a couple of minutes, I moved on.

By now the traffic had eased off. For the first time I noticed that the stars were out. It wasn't quite the Australian night sky, but it was still impressive. A few weeks ago I'd been staring at the stars in Tasmania. I'd told everyone in Australia that I was coming back to care for Bob.

A fine job I've done of that, I cursed myself.

Had my long stay in Australia caused this? Had that time apart loosened the ties between me and Bob? Had it made Bob question my commitment to him? When the Rottweiler had attacked, had he decided that he could no longer rely on me to protect him? The thought made me want to scream.

As Belle's road loomed into view I was close to tears. What was I going to do without him? I'd never find a companion like Bob again.

It was then that it happened. For the

first time in years, I experienced an over-whelming need for a fix.

If I really had lost Bob, I wouldn't be able to cope. I'd have to numb myself from the grief I was already feeling.

I knew Belle's flatmate took drugs. The closer I got to her street, the more terrifying the thoughts in my head were becoming.

It was nearly ten o'clock. I had been wandering the streets for a couple of hours. In the distance, the police sirens were wailing. Perhaps the cops were on their way to another punch-up in a pub. I couldn't have cared less.

As I walked up the path to Belle's dimly lit front entrance, I spotted a shape sitting quietly in the shadows to the side of the building. It was the silhouette of a cat.

I'd given up hope by now. It was probably another stray, sheltering from the cold. But then I saw his face, that unmistakable face.

'Bob.'

He let out a plaintive meow, just like the one in the hallway on the night we first met.

'Where have you been?' he seemed to say. 'I've been waiting here for ages.'

I scooped him up and held him close.

'You are going to be the death of me if you keep running away like that,' I said, my mind scrambling to work out how he'd got here.

Of course! Bob had been to Belle's flat with me several times, and spent six weeks here when I was away. It made sense that he'd come here. I felt a fool for not thinking of it earlier. But how on earth had he done it by himself? It was a mile and a half from the Angel tube station. Had he walked all the way? If so, how long had he been here?

None of that mattered now. As I carried on making a fuss of him, he licked my hand. His tongue was as rough as sandpaper. He rubbed his face against mine and curled his tail.

I ran up to Belle's flat and she invited me in. My mood had been transformed from despair to delirium. I was on top of the world.

'Want something to celebrate?' Belle's flatmate smiled, knowingly.

'No, I'm fine thanks,' I laughed, tugging on Bob as he scratched playfully at my hand.

Bob didn't need drugs to get through

the night. He just needed me. And all I needed was Bob. Not just tonight, but for as long as I had the privilege of having him in my life.

Chapter 30
Bob, The *Big Issue* Cat

As the March sun disappeared and dusk fell, London wound up for the evening once more. The traffic was thick on Islington High Street and the honking of horns was endless. The pavements were busy too, with a stream of people flowing in and out of the station concourse. The rush hour was under way and living up to its name.

I was checking that I had enough papers left when I saw out of the corner of my eye that a group of kids had gathered around us. They were teenagers, three boys and a couple of girls. They looked South American, or maybe Spanish or Portuguese.

There was nothing unusual about this. Islington had its fair share of tourists and Bob was a magnet for them. Barely a day went by without him being surrounded like this.

What was different this evening, however, was the way they were animatedly pointing and talking about him.

'Ah, *si*, Bob,' said one teenage girl.

'*Si, si*. Bob the Beeg Issew Cat,' said another.

Weird, I thought to myself when I realised what she'd said. *How do they know*

*his name is Bob? He doesn't wear a name tag.
And what do they mean by the* Big Issue *Cat?*

'How do you know Bob?' I asked, hoping one of them spoke decent English. My Spanish was non-existent.

'Oh, we see him on YouTube,' one of the boys smiled. 'Bob is very popular, yes?'

'Is he?' I said. 'Someone told me he was on YouTube, but I've got no idea how many people watch it.'

'Many people, I think,' the boy laughed.

'Where are you from?' I asked curiously.

'*España*, Spain.'

'So Bob's popular in Spain?'

'*Si, si,*' another one of the boys said. '*Bob es una estrella en España.* He is a star in Spain.'

I was shocked.

I knew that lots of people had taken photographs of Bob over the years, both while I was busking and now that I was selling the *Big Issue*. I'd jokingly wondered once whether he should be put forward for the *Guinness Book of Records*: the world's most photographed cat.

A couple of people had filmed him too, some with their phones and others with proper video cameras. Who could have shot a film that was now on YouTube?

The following morning I headed down to the local library with Bob and booked myself online.

I punched in the search terms: Bob Big Issue Cat. Sure enough, there was a link to YouTube. I clicked on it. To my surprise there was not one, but two films there.

'Hey Bob, look, he was right. You are a star on YouTube.'

Bob hadn't been terribly interested until that point. It wasn't Channel Four racing, after all. But when I clicked on the first video and he saw and heard me talking, Bob jumped on to the keyboard and popped his face right up against the screen.

The first film was called 'Bobcat and I'. A memory came back to me. A film student followed me around for a while back during the days when we were selling the *Big Issue* in Covent Garden. There was nice footage of me and Bob there, getting on the bus and walking the streets. The film summarised the day-to-day life of a *Big Issue* seller pretty well.

The other video was more recent, and had been filmed around the Angel by a

Russian guy. I clicked on the link. He'd called his film 'Bob The *Big Issue* Cat'. This must have been the one that the Spanish students had seen. It had had tens of thousands of hits. I was gobsmacked.

Bob was becoming a proper celebrity.

This wasn't a complete surprise. It had been building for a while. Every now and again someone would say: 'Ah, is that Bob? I've heard about him.' Or 'Is this the famous Bobcat?' Then, a few weeks before meeting the Spanish teenagers, we had featured in a local newspaper, the *Islington Tribune*. I'd even been approached by an American lady, an agent.

'Have you ever thought about writing a book about you and Bob?' she had asked.

As if!

But meeting the Spanish teenagers showed me that Bob's fame had grown more than I realised. He was becoming a feline star.

I couldn't help smiling.

'Bob saved my life,' I had said on one of the films.

When I first heard that, I thought it sounded a bit crass, a bit of an exaggeration. But as Bob and I left the library and walked along the road, it began to sink in: it was true, he really had.

In the two years since I'd found him sitting in that half-lit hallway, Bob had transformed my world. I'd been a recovering heroin addict, living a hand-to-mouth existence. I was in my late twenties with no direction or purpose in life beyond survival. I'd lost contact with my family and barely had a friend in the world. My life was a total mess. Now all that had changed.

My trip to Australia hadn't made up for the difficulties of the past, but it had brought me and my mother back together again. The wounds were healing. I hoped that my battle with drugs was finally drawing to a close. The day when I wouldn't even have to take Subutex was looming on the horizon. I could finally see an end to my addiction. There had been times when I'd never imagined that was possible.

Most of all, I'd laid down some roots. My little flat in Tottenham had given me the kind of security and stability that I'd always craved. I'd been living there longer than anywhere I'd ever been. I was sure that none of it would have happened without Bob.

I'm not a Buddhist, but I like Buddhist philosophies. They give you a very good structure that you can build your life around. Karma, for instance: the idea that what goes around, comes around. I wondered whether Bob was my reward for having done something good, somewhere in my troubled life.

Perhaps Bob and I had known each other in a previous life. Our bond, our instant connection was very unusual.

'You two are the reincarnation of Dick Whittington and his cat!' someone said to me once.

Except it felt as if Dick Whittington had come back as Bob, and I as his companion. I liked that thought.

Bob is my best mate, the one who has

guided me towards a different – and a better – way of life. He doesn't demand anything complicated in return. He just needs me to take care of him. And that's what I do.

The road ahead wasn't going to be smooth. We were sure to face our problems here and there – I was still working on the streets of London, after all. It was never going to be easy. But as long as we were together, I had a feeling it was going to be fine.

Everybody needs a break. Everybody deserves that second chance. Bob and I had taken ours . . .

Acknowledgements

Writing this book has been an amazing experience. Lots of people have played their part.

First and foremost I'd like to thank my family, and my Mum and Dad in particular, for giving me the determination that has kept me going through some dark times in my life. I'd also like to thank my godparents, Terry and

ACKNOWLEDGEMENTS

Merilyn Winters, for being such great friends to me.

On the streets of London, so many people have shown kindness to me over the years, but I'd like to single out Sam, Tom, Lee and Rita, the *Big Issue* co-ordinators who have been so generous to me. I'd also like to thank outreach workers Kevin and Chris for their compassion and understanding. Thanks also to the Blue Cross and RSPCA for their valuable advice and to Davika, Leanne and the rest of the staff at Angel tube station who have been so supportive of me and Bob.

I'd also like to thank Food For Thought and Pix in Neal Street who have always offered me and Bob a warm cup of tea and a saucer of milk, as well as Daryl at Diamond Jacks in Soho and Paul and

Den the cobblers who have always been my good friends. I'd like also to mention Pete Watkins at Corrupt Drive Records, DJ Cavey Nik at Mosaic Homes, Ron Richardson and Peter Gruner of the Islington Tribune who was the first person to write about Bob and I five years ago.

This book would never have happened if it hadn't been for my agent Mary Pachnos. She's the one who first approached me with the idea. It sounded pretty crazy at the time, and I'd never have been able to get it all down and turned into a coherent story without the help of her and the writer Garry Jenkins. So a heartfelt thanks to both Mary and Garry. At my publishers, Hodder & Stoughton, I'd like to thank Rowena Webb, Ciara Foley, Emma Knight and the rest of the brilliant team there. Also thanks to Lucy Courtenay who did a brilliant job abridging this edition. Thanks also to Alan and the staff at Waterstone's in Islington who even let me and Garry work on the book in the quiet upstairs. And a big thank you to Kitty. Without her constant support, we'd both be lost.

Finally I'd like to thank Scott Hartford-Davis and the Dalai Lama who have, in recent years, given me a great philosophy by which to live my life.

Last, and most definitely not least, of course, I have to thank the little fellow who came into my life in 2007 and who – from the moment I befriended him – has proven to be such a positive, life-changing force in my life. Everyone deserves a friend like Bob. I have been very fortunate indeed to have found one . . .

James Bowen
London, October 2012

Bob Information Page

Read the latest news and stories from
James and Bob at www.hodder.co.uk
and at Bob's very own Twitter site:
@streetcatbob